Antelope Running

To: Cary, Chuck, Johnny,
Thank you for years
of kindness & TLC
for me & all my cats!

God Bless!
Merry Christmas
best of new years
Betty W. Smith

Antelope Running

Betty Walker-Smith

Outskirts Press, Inc.
Denver, Colorado

Outskirts Press, Inc.
http://www.outskirtspress.com

ISBN: 978-1-4327-5686-4

Outskirts Press and the "OP" logo are trademarks belonging to Outskirts Press, Inc.

PRINTED IN THE UNITED STATES OF AMERICA

TO MY MOM and DAD,
Ollie Ray (Ted) and Erma Walker

Why do I want to write this story? I do not want it to just be a narrative of events, or just a memoir or travelogue. I want to write it because I think my family and friends will enjoy it. And I want to write it because these experiences are well worth remembering.

Table of Contents

1

Teaching On The Navajo Reservation

This Southwest that drew me here to New Mexico and Arizona when I was just out of college in the early 1960's was a perfect place, the place I was supposed to be. I cannot forget the drive west of Albuquerque with those blue mesas that are sometimes salmon-colored, sometimes purple – beautiful against a sky so blue it almost seems turquoise. I believe the Native American cultures that inhabited these enchanting lands sensed the unique beauty of their surroundings. It certainly shows up in their artwork with the little rounded clouds in the blue skies.

Driving west from Chinle, Arizona toward the village of Pinon where I taught my first year, is a gorgeous scene with the dark blue or black mesas silhouetted against the evening sky. The area is called Black Mesa. It seems the spirit of the people and the silent beauty of the land are inseparable.

This small settlement of Pinon, Arizona is about thirty-seven miles west of Chinle, Arizona. Chinle is near the New Mexico border in the northeastern part of Arizona. I did not even realize there were places like this that still existed. Sometimes, it was as if

ANTELOPE RUNNING

I were not living in the United States. The school where I taught and the trading post along with housing for school staff made up the community. My memories are filled with the variety of people on the staff — the one white-haired older lady and another lady from Ohio whom I will call Ginny. She was one of those people you considered yourself lucky to meet. We shared a small apartment. There was also the guy who came later as the PE teacher. I still remember P. out on the playground with the little Navajos. He was tall, handsome, blond and had a quiet shyness that made him very charming.

X Places I taught
● Places mentioned
  in text

A SOUTHWEST TEACHING ADVENTURE

TEACHING ON THE NAVAJO RESERVATION

I taught second grade that first year. The children came to school speaking very little English. I did not have any training in teaching English as a Second Language at that time. The children were very shy, so my work was cut out for me. In their culture, they try not to stand out above their peers. I remember going over the little "Weekly Reader" that ran a story about the Russian Sputnik satellite. I am sure they did not understand anything about it. Though I am not a good artist, I drew rough diagrams on the blackboard telling them about this object going around the sky that could be used to send messages.

The children were eager to learn, and they were not a big discipline problem. I tried to teach them some songs. I made a chart with the words of "The Happy Wanderer" and "Val de Re, Val de Rah," but that was an unsuccessful effort. I played a record of The Kingston Trio singing "Michael, Row the Boat Ashore," and that worked better. I still get tears in my eyes when I hear that song.

We had a woman principal and an assistant who had years of experience working near Chinle; they did their best to be helpful. We were on duty year-round, except for vacation time in the summer and time off to attend a university to work on advanced degrees. We might be asked to help paint a classroom during this time.

That first summer after my first year, the principal sent me out with two Navajo dormitory employees to recruit students for the next school year. There was no compulsory attendance law at that time in 1963. That is an experience I hope I never forget. We went to one little boy's grandmother's summer home. It was a shelter called a ramada which consisted of four log posts at corners supporting a roof of branches covered with leaves.

ANTELOPE RUNNING

Under this was a bed and a cookstove. I can't remember if it was propane stove or if it burned wood—probably the latter. It was a warm, summer day, and the grandmother spoke broken English, but was kind and gentle. I grew to love the quiet strength of the Navajo people. During the eight years I worked on the Navajo Reservation, I do not recall hearing any of them lose their temper or yell.

After we signed up little Edwin, the dorm attendants took me to a "sheep dip." A sheep dip is a place where the sheep are dipped in a trough of water with some chemical – I think it was creosote – to kill the insects in their wool. This was another adventure. I recall an old Navajo man riding around on his beautiful horse as if he were supervising the operation; he wore his long black hair in the traditional style tied up with white yarn in a double knot behind.

One evening Ms. Brinkley, the principal, took a couple of us greenhorns out to visit Mr. Yazzie, a member of the school board. He lived in a hogan, the traditional home of the Navajo. It was a hexagonal structure built of stacked logs with mud chinked between. There was a small stove in the center with pipe going out through a hole in the roof. Pieces of art – beautiful handwoven Navajo rugs – hung on the wall and we sat around in a circle on some other rugs. I would have a problem now sitting on the floor like that.

Other unforgettable times included trips over to Chinle, Arizona where I met my new friend, Vi, who taught at a school to the north. Sometimes we went to the small community church there on Sunday morning and then ate lunch at the beautiful Thunderbird Lodge. The small room was lovely with huge cottonwood vigas (logs) in the ceiling. The trading post next door was piled high with gorgeous Navajo rugs. This lovely old room was where Vi met her future husband. We were having dinner there, and so was he.

After lunch we sometimes went to Canyon de Chelley, a mystic canyon nearby. I still return there periodically as it seems to call me back. The pale sandstone cliffs rise hundreds of feet – some up to 800 feet. The first time we went, we rented horses and rode in on a perfectly warm Sunday afternoon. I could not possibly say which was more breathtakingly beautiful – sunrise or sunset in this canyon of the Southwestern United States with its French name, Canyon de Chelley (Shay).

As we rode in on this lazy, summer day so long ago, we were met by several Navajos riding out. I will never forget the old gentleman in front. His ancient, tanned face was marked with the deep lines of time and he seemed to blend with the timeless, eroded shapes of the canyon. Perched above his kindly, old face was a dilapidated, misshapen cowboy hat, which he tipped to us. He looked like a model for a Laura Gilpin photograph. Laura Gilpin did classic photography of Native Americans.

This area is more than six thousand feet in elevation The August day was quite pleasant as we rode horseback into this flat canyon. The wide, sandy bottom made for a lovely ride for both horse and rider. The huge, rocky cliffs ranged in color from eggshell to almost ochre. They appeared to rise up to meet the turquoise blue sky. If you know where to look, there are numerous pictographs and petroglyphs on the canyon walls. These are a type of record drawn on the rock walls. The ancient people believed if they drew a picture of the animal they were hunting, they were likely to kill it. Pictographs were painted, while petroglyphs were just carved.

ANTELOPE RUNNING

On another visit to this enchanted place, we were on the rim at sunset. It was one of those serendipitous sights that become etched as a treasure in one's mind. It was the "off season" for tourists, so my friend and I were the only human beings for miles. We walked up and down along the rim and explored various rock formations, trying to view the canyon from all possible angles.

Softly, as in a dream, I heard the melodic tinkle of a little bell. Was I in a Buddhist temple in the Orient or in a wild and beautiful place in the United States? It was the tiny bell on a goat that was leading a flock of sheep hundreds of feet below us. This was one of the most amazing and beautiful aspects of living and working on the Navajo Reservation. Often it seemed as if I were on another continent – a unique and gorgeous continent.

While Navajo families keep their summer homes in the bottom of the canyon, they move out in winter because of the snow. They grow peach trees and herd their sheep down there. A scenic drive around the canyon rim is one thing everyone likes to do. It seemed this was one of the few places left in America where time had not rushed by like a monster swallowing up tranquility.

One beautiful weekend, my sister, Hazel, and husband, Cecil came to visit me in Albuquerque. We went to Canyon de Chelly for a brief visit. I remember Hazel picking up a beautiful piece of driftwood. I also took other sisters and friends there. Hazel and Cecil have both passed away.

This lonely land, so beautiful in its desolation, was not the type of place I could have envisioned myself when I was young. But God in his omnipotence knew where I could best start the journey toward finding myself. He knew that I would make a better beginning while viewing the dazzling sunsets and the softness of the twilight on the silent mesas, sometimes glowing with mauve, peach and smoky blue strokes of the Great Artist himself. These sunsets could never be captured in their full, tranquilizing beauty in either a photograph or a painting. They must be witnessed personally.

Another unforgettable scene happened years later when my husband and I drove west on I-40 somewhere in northern Arizona. In the dusk of a late autumn evening, a lone barren tree was silhouetted against the flaming orange of a sun that did not want to disappear from the horizon. It reminded me of an Oriental painting. Just as the Navajos are continually drawn back to their homeland, as if by a powerful magnet, I, too, periodically feel compelled to journey back to this mysterious, desolate place.

Later, on one of my return trips I took a photograph from about that same viewpoint on the canyon rim. It is enlarged and hangs in my living room now as one of my prized possessions. I have even sold copies of it and given it for presents.

On Halloween night in 1962, we held a Carnival at the Pinon Boarding School where I worked. My friend, Vi, came over to help. The next morning we awoke and left for the Arizona State Teachers Convention in Phoenix. We never made it as we had an accident a few miles west of a Dairy Queen in Winslow on old Highway 66. Vi's little Volkswagen bug flipped over on an old gravel shoulder. She and I were thrown out and landed in the shallow ditch. Thank the good Lord it was not deep. A principal from Chinle Elementary School was right behind us and saw everything. He flagged down oncoming traffic so someone could call an ambulance from the hospital in Winslow. Some find it hard to believe, including me, but there were two excellent physicians in that small town: Dr. B, a surgeon, and Dr. P., an orthopedist. Both our necks were broken, but they put us back together. Is that a miracle or what?

We were in the hospital for five weeks. Both our mothers came out to be with us. My brother, Dick, paid my mom's airfare to fly to Phoenix where she caught a small Frontier shuttle up to Winslow. A lady named Mrs. Greer who had worked at the hospital lived about a block away. She invited both our moms to stay with her as she had an extra bedroom. During the five weeks the three of them became the best of friends. My principal and her assistant were very kind to us as they came and visited us in the hospital. They helped fill out the volumes of forms necessary because we were on government time. When I was released from the hospital, it was near Christmas and my mom and I went back to my home in Dallas on the train. I wore a neck brace for about two months and went back to teaching after Christmas vacation.

The summer of 1963 Vi and I decided to attend Arizona State University in Tempe, Arizona near Phoenix to pursue our Masters. We shared an apartment where, of course, it was very hot. We ran from one air-conditioned building to another. I still remember going into Goldwater's Department Store after having lived out in the "boonies" for a year. It was as if I had never been in a beautiful store: I kept saying, "Oh! Look at this!!! Isn't this beautiful?"

In 1963, a new school had just been built at Crownpoint, New Mexico. Vi and I asked for a transfer there. The administration did not want to give it to us, but we used the excuse of our health needs because of the accident, and they finally agreed. I taught fourth grade there and she taught third. It was a much bigger school than where I had been at Pinon. There were about eight hundred children that first year with thirty one teachers. Many of us were young and idealistic. I was there four years from 1963 to 1967.

The next summer I transferred from Arizona State in boiling Phoenix to Northern Arizona University in Flagstaff where it was cooler. I earned a Masters' Degree in Elementary Education. I became familiar with a new program called "Language Experiences in Reading." This method emphasized getting the children to write stories using the vocabulary words from their reading text. It worked quite well, teaching the word "striped" as in a shirt. We wrote a story about a cowboy with a striped shirt. This was a familiar concept in their culture and helped to develop the idea. I am sure I drew a crude picture on the board showing stripes. We were carefully supervised every year by the principal, an assistant, or someone from the Bureau of Indian Affairs headquarters in Window Rock, Arizona.

These supervisors came into the classroom and observed the teaching. Then they wrote a report and the teacher was called into the office to discuss what went on. Sometimes we were notified of the upcoming visit and sometimes not. One day, I remember looking up and seeing a bunch of supervisors in my class, including my principal and other supervisors from Window Rock. There was quite a hierarchy of administrators at that time.

In the summer of 1964 Vi and I were chosen to be the demonstration teachers for the "New Teacher Orientation." Vi was the main teacher and I was the assistant or substitute. The administration had learned after our accident in 1962 that they should have a "stand-in" just in case. Vi and I decided to present our "unit" on "Communication." The "unit" method of teaching was quite in vogue at that time. The idea has returned to middle schools and high schools as the block method. It involves correlating all your subjects around one central theme in Language Arts, Science, Social Studies and Math.

We were still benefiting from the education support of "The Kennedy Years," which provided sufficient money for education. The plan was to bring the children to Albuquerque on the train and stay in a motel. We did this and took our class to visit the *Albuquerque Journal* where they watched the huge printing presses roll out the newspaper. We also visited one of the television stations, where we were on TV for about two seconds. It was quite an adventure for all of us, most of all, for the little Navajo third graders. When we returned the students wrote stories about the trip. We integrated math with the number of miles we traveled, the number of meals we ate and the cost. We covered social studies with a map of New Mexico showing Crownpoint, the route traveled and Albuquerque.

One summer day Vi and I were driving north from Crownpoint on our way to Denver. It was hot and dry and the car was not air-conditioned. We stopped to get out and stretch and have a drink of water, as the road was tiring since it was unpaved and rough. As we stood there, north of us, maybe about a mile, a herd of antelope were running across the desert. I felt as if I were in a movie.

When I was promoted to the job of Education Specialist, I worked out of the superintendent's office. My responsibilities included visiting the small outlying schools where the younger children could live at home; I helped the teachers with reading and language instruction. I still remember the elementary schools in Mariano Lake, Standing Rock and Borrego Pass. These schools usually only went up to third grade. The teachers in these remote locations were usually quite dedicated; I became friends with some.

TEACHING ON THE NAVAJO RESERVATION

I remember one special day when I was assigned to visit Borrego Pass. The road out southeast from Crownpoint was unpaved, and it had snowed the night before. As is often the case in New Mexico, clouds had disappeared and the sun was shining brightly, glistening on the fresh snow. My government car suddenly bogged down in the muddy slush. I was completely stuck! I got out and walked around the car but couldn't figure out how to get it unstuck. In a few minutes I saw a Navajo man walking across the field; he helped me get moving again. This was yet another example of the kind, gentle nature of these people whom I grew to love and respect. I believe that they were glad teachers were willing to come out to teach their children. I believe this helpful attitude reminded me of the kind, country people I knew as a child growing up in North Texas.

At the time I came out, the Bureau of Indian Affairs sent recruiters around the country to various colleges and universities to encourage new graduates to sign up. A Mr. E. C. came to McMurry College in Abilene, Texas, where I did my undergraduate work. He was there in the spring of 1962 and my girlfriend, Marcia, and I signed up to come out to the Navajo Reservation to teach. She changed her mind, but I obviously did not. In the summer of 1962, I headed to Gallup. I did not have a car, so I traveled on a Greyhound bus. I had shipped my clothes and other possessions ahead to the Personnel Office in Gallup.

I still remember the telegram I received explaining where they would meet me; I had never received a telegram before. I was taken out to a boarding school at Ft. Wingate near Gallup. We had two weeks of orientation, which included Navajo history and culture. On the Friday night of the second week, they took us to a Navajo "Squaw Dance." This is a social dance to help the young people meet each other. The young girls asked the guys to dance. If one of the boys did not want to dance with the girl who asked, he had to pay her a quarter. The dance was held outdoors around a campfire on a lovely summer evening. When the dance was over, VI and I went camping with friends at McGaffey Lake nearby.

The next Monday we reported to Chinle Boarding School. There we had two more weeks of training before we were sent out to our schools – Pinon Boarding School for me. While we were there, we took another weekend camping trip north of Chinle, near Lukachukai. The beautiful Buffalo Pass camping area was so high we could see across the plains into the Shiprock New Mexico area. The camping area was green and beautiful, the juniper trees contrasting with the reddish, orange sandstone mesas.

The last Sunday before we were to report to our schools, we took a fellow teacher to Tuba City, Arizona several miles north of the Grand Canyon. We traveled west through the Hopi Mesas, as we wanted to visit Old Oraibi, the third mesa. The stillness of the place was striking. The only sounds were a dog barking in the distance and the soft tone of an Indian drum on the bright Sunday morning. We also attended a snake dance at one of the Hopi Mesas. We watched from the roof of one of their adobe houses; this is where I wanted to be as one dancer draped a rattlesnake around his neck, holding and stroking it. The Hopi Pueblo villages date back hundreds of years; the people are known for their beautiful pottery and kachina dolls. Kachina dolls were carved from wood and were supposed to represent spirits.

In 1966, I had a chance to go to Europe on a college tour with

Northern Arizona University at Flagstaff. My superintendent, Miss C., thought it would be a good educational experience since the title of the tour was "A Comparative Study of European and American Educational Systems." It was yet another one of my fantastic adventures.

Article from the *Crownpoint News*, April 6, 1966

Miss Betty Walker (now Betty Walker Smith), a former teacher at Crownpoint Boarding School and now employed at the Agency Education Office as Education Specialist, has been selected by the Board of Advisory Editors to appear in the 1965 Edition of OUTSTANDING YOUNG WOMEN of AMERICA. McMurry College of Abilene, Texas, recommended her for this honor.

Miss Walker has also been selected by the Northern Arizona University of Flagstaff to be a member of a group which will tour Europe this summer (1966). The tour is sponsored by the University for the purpose of visiting European school systems. She will visit Copenhagen, Amsterdam, West Berlin, Vienna, Paris, Rome and London. She will leave New York City on July 9 by Royal Dutch Jet Airlines for Copenhagen. She will be returning to the United States the latter part of August.

Miss Walker is a former Texas Resident. She is a graduate of Van Alstyne High School and McMurry College. Before attending college, Miss Walker was employed by a cotton exporting company as secretary and in Washington, D.C. with the Defense Department. She has been a Red Cross volunteer and in 1965, she received a Special Service Award from the Bureau of Indian Affairs. While working at the Boarding School, Miss

ANTELOPE RUNNING

Walker was active in the Girl Scout Program at the school. She is a member of the Crownpoint Methodist Church.

Betty with Girl Scouts @ Crownpoint Boadring School

2

The Isleta Pueblo Adventure

One of my supervisors on the Navajo Reservation received a promotion to principal at Isleta Elementary School located at the Isleta Pueblo, about fifteen miles south of Albuquerque. My husband and I had wanted to move to Albuquerque and buy a home, since we could not buy property on the Reservation. We had spent the last few years in government housing that was provided for staff for a small rental fee. Mr. M., the new Isleta Principal, told me that if I ever wanted to come to Albuquerque, to let him know. In late 1969, I applied for a transfer to Isleta, and it was approved. We moved into an apartment in southeast Albuquerque, and I commuted to Isleta every school day.

Isleta was another rewarding experience. I had quite a few friends among the staff, and I also became friends with parents and others at the Pueblo. We have so much to learn from the Native Americans as they came to be called. They are, in most cases, a very sincere, gentle people. I have pieces of pottery which were gifts from the children, aides and parents. I also have beautiful turquoise jewelry I received from the children as Christmas presents. They were in little, miniature treasure chests.

ANTELOPE RUNNING

My mom passed away in 1983 and I received this card:

THE ISLETA PUEBLO ADVENTURE

Dear Mrs. Smith,

I'm sorry to hear the bad news about your mother and I wish I could be there. We all miss you. I hope your mother went to heaven. I hope she had a great time on earth. May her soul Rest in peace. Wish you were here.

from Tom,

This school applied for and received Title I funds because of the students' difficulty with English. My first year at Isleta, another teacher and I were asked to write the Title 1 grant. Title 1 is a special government program for bi-lingual education. With the grant, every class was supported with a teacher's aide. The assistants were usually Isleta women who were invaluable since they were familiar with the culture.

Language Master was a recording machine that used a card about 10" x 4" with recording tape across the top. My aide wrote the new vocabulary words from each story in the reading text and I recorded the corresponding words on the card. The cards were kept in labeled shoeboxes in order on the table where I had three separate groups every day. The children were assigned to listen to the new words with earphones after I had introduced the vocabulary from the cards.

ANTELOPE RUNNING

Some of the aides were quite artistic. One woman I worked with for a number of years was great at decorating our classrooms for Christmas. I had seen the beautifully designed Pueblo style fireplaces in museums, so I asked her to draw a corner fireplace like that with some native pottery sitting on the shelf on top. She did it exactly as I asked and then enlarged it on the overhead projector to bulletin board size, and that was the center of our Christmas decorations. The aides also cut strips of red and green crepe paper which we twisted to give it a curly look. We strung the strips between light fixtures and hung icicles along the strips. Luckily, we never started a fire.

Before so many restrictions, another year at Christmas, I decided to do the Christmas story from the Bible for an assembly program. Each class was supposed to do one program every year. The aides were also a great help with the program. We had three students dress as wise men in men's robes and blankets. They carried "gifts of frankincense and myrrh" in tissue boxes covered with gold and red paper. The little boy shepherds wore jeans with beautiful native, white, lacy shirts over red, long-sleeved style shirts. They carried broomstick staffs covered with brown crepe paper. The little angels were dressed in white.

The Nativity scene included Mary and Joseph beside a little wooden manger that was made by a custodian who used real straw. Another year, one of my aides borrowed a traditional cradle from an uncle. It was made from small sticks. The custodian hung it from the ceiling in the auditorium, which was quite an operation; this was the way it was done long ago. Our school building was a fifty-year-old adobe and the ceiling in the auditorium was quite high. A little dark-eyed, brown-skinned nine-year-old girl played Mary. I am sure she looked more like the real Mary than any of the Madonnas ever painted. My aide brought a gorgeous blue chiffon scarf which we draped around her face. A shy, handsome little boy stood beside her as Joseph.

One year, my aide translated Luke, Chapter 2: Verses 8 – 11 into the native Tewa language. She read it that way as part of the program. The class painted a huge mural to hang across the back of the stage. It had the dark blue and purple sky with many stars, one much brighter than the rest. I asked them to paint their own village down below. It was so adorable with the little adobe houses with tiny strands of red chiles hanging on the doorways. I still have a picture of that beautiful Nativity scene.

ANTELOPE RUNNING

②

afraid.
pei may

And the angel said unto them,
An-he-le tha ba e oo bae may ms

"Fear not for behold I bring
wea pe che (Yan noo)

you good tidings of great joy,
mum na bab-oo) ka cha mi'tle (shim

Which shall be to all people.
ba di-nin noom-i-) shim ba 'ma
(people)

For unto you is born this day
wea ee num' i, (you-the (wim-a) oo-oo-thea)
+his day)

in the city of David, a savior,
oo - wa bun you thea 'na ba he, hun

Which is Christ, the Lord
i Davi Kee-Ha

Translation from the Bible in English to Tewa Language of Isleta Pueblo

I taught fourth and fifth grades for most of my fourteen years at Isleta. In the 1970s we began to have open classrooms and non-graded programs. One summer four of us teachers from Isleta were sent to the University of Colorado at Boulder for a month-long training to develop this idea. It was a fabulous experience. That fall we came back and started the program with our fourth, fifth and sixth graders. I remember making individual packets to help each child complete at his or her own pace. One packet focused on the vital organs of the human body. The child had to draw each organ on construction paper and put it in the correct position where it is located in the body diagram. The packet included diagrams and pictures for instruction.

I always held a book club where I encouraged the children to create their own little library at home. We belonged to a Club where I received a catalog every month. Each child got a sheet that listed the available books. They took their lists home and made their selections with their parents. They brought back the 25 or 50 cents for the paperbacks and I sent in the order. It was always exciting when the order came back and I could pass out their new purchases. If the children got a card from the public library, they received a special "surprise."

In the classroom, we had a library where the children could check out books. My aide kept a year-long record of the books each child read. When a student returned a book, we asked about the characters and plot to make sure the student had read the book. At the end of the year, the child who had read the most books, received a beautiful, museum-type book on Indian culture.

I also had a year-long contest where children competed to have the most new vocabulary words. The children listed new words they encountered from anywhere they chose. They wrote definitions and pronunciations beside each word. They kept their lists in their notebooks. The child with the most words received a gorgeous National Geographic book on Indian life at the end of the year.

ANTELOPE RUNNING

We held bake sales through the year to pay for the Indian culture books and other expenses. We usually had a field trip to town once a year. The school paid for the bus gas, but if we wanted to go to a movie or museum or get pizza, we had to pay ourselves. Since most of the children could not afford all that, we raised the money ourselves. The parents were always so willing to make cupcakes and Rice Crispies bars for the sale.

One year, we went to Albuquerque to see the movie, "American Wilderness." The photography was outstanding and the children loved it. In the days following, I conducted language activities related to the move, since it motivated them to write. In one of the activities, I asked the children to name all the animals in the movie (nouns). I wrote the list on the blackboard. Then I asked them to tell me what the animals were doing (verbs). Next we described the animals (adjectives). Last, we made sentences using the parts of speech. I'll never forget the picture and short paragraph that one little girl created. She drew a picture of a blue river with lots of fish. In her story she wrote about how "the fish go to school."

I also tried to get the children interested in a hobby. One beautiful, spring day, we had a hobby day out under the trees. Tables were set up and I brought my rock collection, and some children brought along their collections. One little girl brought me a beautiful geode, a picture agate that looks like a remote beach scene – as might be seen along the Baja Peninsula in Mexico. I asked her where she got it and she said by the mesa to the west of the Pueblo.

In the early 1980's I decided that there was so much artistic talent there that we should have an Art Show. I brought it up at a staff meeting, and we organized committees. We did it! We made a huge banner to hang out in front to advertise it. Each teacher had the classes draw or paint pictures. These were hung on the hallway walls. One little girl who was taking piano lessons played for us at the program. My class dramatized one of the Grimm Brothers Fairy Tales, "The Bremen Town Musicians." The aides made up nice programs listing the various activities. We also asked one of the elders to come in and tell stories to the children.

Examples of Children's Art

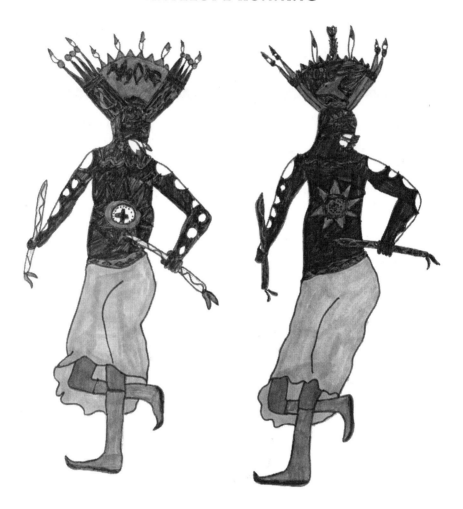

Apache Dancers

Around the late 1970's we had quite a different event at Isleta Elementary School. A former opera singer came to our school to do a program with the children to introduce them to "Opera." The singer's name was Bonnie Jo Hunt, a Native American of the Lakota Sioux Tribe. She had sung with the Paris and the San Francisco Operas.

THE ISLETA PUEBLO ADVENTURE

Teachers were informed in advance about this opportunity; we told our classes about it and asked for volunteers who would like to participate in doing a scene from an opera. I had two or three volunteers from my class. We met with Bonnie Jo and practiced the scene with her singing the part. She had brought costumes for the children. It was a completely new experience for them.

Some years later when I was hiking with my Sunday afternoon group from the New Mexico Mountain Club, Bonnie Jo was in the group. She became a regular member, and we became friends.

At that time she was working with teachers on the Navajo Reservation helping the children to overcome some of their shyness and gain self-confidence. Bonnie Jo used her experience performing on stage by helping teachers and children put on a variety show. She had a team of people who worked with her. One was a male dancer from Zuni Pueblo who taught the little boys to do the Hoop Dance. Other children learned little songs and performed in groups. They were dressed in appropriate costumes to fit the music.

I went a few times with my camera and two of Bonnie Jo's. We formed a group of upper grade children who were interested in photography. The scenery was beautiful, especially around Kayenta Elementary School next door to Monument Valley with the huge volcanic plugs. We went out two weeks before the program was scheduled to practice with the children. I took the small group of four or five children, and we took pictures. I brought them back to Albuquerque and had slides made.

When we went back in two weeks to do the program, I met with the "photographers," and we wrote the script for each slide. Then, the slides were shown as part of the variety show with the participating children reading the script. Once when we went to Crownpoint Boarding School where I taught in the 1960's, one of my former students was a teacher there. She remembered me, and we had a wonderful reunion. I met her family that evening at the program, and we took pictures.

Another great part of teaching at Isleta was two other teachers that I met there in the late 70's. I carpooled with both of them at different times. One was a Black woman named Emma. She was one of the most kind, gentle people I have ever known. She lived in Albuquerque, almost on my way to Isleta, as I lived in the northern part, and, so, I picked her up. She was a joyful person and a delight to be around. She later developed severe rheumatoid arthritis and suffered for several years. She was very close to God, and when I went to visit, her Bible was always near her recliner. I still miss her as she said that she always prayed for me.

The other teacher was Nita. She usually picked me up since she lived east of me. She was another gentle soul. Nita and her husband, John had several children. She always had a big Thanksgiving dinner. Since I had no family in Albuquerque, I spent quite a number of those wonderful holiday dinners with Nita, her husband and family. They welcomed me as if I were a part of their family.

Nita was always helpful. Shortly after I bought new furniture for my living room, she told me about a garage sale up the street from their lovely home. I ran over there quickly and bought a very nice Oriental table lamp that went perfectly with my new furniture.

⌒⌒

My experience teaching on the Indian reservations was an adventure of a lifetime.

THE ISLETA PUEBLO ADVENTURE

There were so many beautiful, exciting times as well as very challenging-but-rewarding times. I now regret that I did not keep a journal. The Bureau of Indian Affairs has received plenty of bad press about conditions in the boarding schools. This may have been justified in the early years. During those times, there was no emphasis on maintaining respect for the native languages and culture, which are intricately intertwined. When the Treaty was signed in 1868 between the U.S. government and the Navajos, education of the children was part of that Agreement.

The philosophy of the responsibility of educating the Indian children seems to have been to "make little white people" out of them. In retrospect, it seems that those in charge should have known that this would not work. After the Navajos were isolated and starved out in Canyon de Chelley, they were taken on "The Long Walk" to Ft. Sumner in eastern New Mexico where an attempt was made to make farmers out of them. Many died on the "Long Walk" and at Ft. Sumner. Finally they were allowed to return to their homeland in western New Mexico and eastern Arizona where they remain today. This is where I taught for eight years, starting at Pinon in Arizona and then at Crownpoint and Tohatchi in New Mexico. The "Long Walk" was similar to the "Trail of Tears" where the Cherokees were driven from North Carolina to Oklahoma.

I believe it is quite regrettable that our Anglo-American culture has not chosen to learn from the varied, positive aspects of Native American cultures. They retain a certain quiet dignity, even after all that has been taken from them. They were the first environmentalists as they only used nature for their individual needs of food, clothing and shelter. They did not exploit it for profit. They knew instinctively that their survival depended on the land, so they worshiped "The Great Spirit" and the rain and sun gods. They thanked him for their livelihood. When I have traveled the west in Rocky Mountain National Park in Colorado, Yosemite in California, Olympic National Park in Washington, and the Grand Canyon, I have thought about all the majesty and beauty of it and that, if I had been an Indian, I would have fought for it, too. I think it is tragic that many tribes have been wiped out. Also, it's tragic that so many treaties that the tribes made in good faith have been broken.

There were so many wonderful times when I worked out there at Isleta Pueblo. I was invited to the Feast Day celebrations and dances. After the dance in the plaza in front of the historic old St. Augustine Church that was built in the 1600s, I was invited over to one of my children's parent's homes for the Feast. The food was a mixture of Anglo-American dishes as well as their native dishes. I felt very honored and hope that I never forget those dancers, men, women and children dressed in their colorful costumes.

The men wore the cotton skirts with the woven, wool belts and necklaces of abalone sea shells, evidence of trading with coastal tribes and Mexican natives. Tropical bird feathers from Mexico have been found in our caves here in New Mexico, proof of trading with these tribes. For some dances they tied pine boughs around their arms. In one of the fall dances the men walk into the Village from the south. The women wore long black dresses made of wool cut across the shoulder with a blouse underneath and colorful scarves tied around their necks. Both the men and women wear beautiful deerskin moccasins. The women's are usually high and come up under their knees.

November 1st is the beginning of deer hunting season, so I always knew little boys would be absent on that day. Their fathers took them to the mountains hunting as part of the ritual of their cultural training. Since prehistoric times, the boys have received orientation into the native ways with ceremonies in the kiva. The kiva is a round building that originally was partially underground. It serves as the center of their rituals. Girls and women were not allowed in the kivas. These buildings always had a ladder sticking out through a hole in the top. I was not allowed to even take a picture of it.

The New Mexico State Capitol is built in a round shape, just like the kiva. When I came to New Mexico in 1962, the state was called "the land of three cultures" – the Indian, the Spanish and the Anglos. We do not talk about it like that anymore since so may other nationalities now reside here.

Another memory of working at Isleta Elementary School was when they acquired a new library building, one of those Butler buildings, which was a metal structure. The underpinning had not yet been added. One morning I went in to get some filmstrips for my class. The librarian said, "Hey, Betty, would you like a puppy?" I said, "Maybe. Ray and I have been looking at pet stores." She pointed to the back where there were two darling puppies eating their breakfast. The mother dog had come under the new library building and had her babies on a frosty October morning.

I immediately chose the cutest one. The mother was part collie and had a pointed nose, a rather long body and long hair. Her puppy was tan with a white face and short hair. Just adorable. He was a plump, little ball of fur. The librarian and her bus driver boyfriend had done a wonderful job helping the stray mom take care of the puppies. I brought him home in a cardboard box.

He already had big feet as a pup, and so Ray and I decided to name him Big Foot. I had been reading stories to my fourth graders about "Sasquatch" and "The Abominable Snowman," but I could not imagine calling "Hey Sasquatch, come here."

Ray and I just loved him, and he was so smart. When he was about ten moths old, we took him to obedience training, since we could tell he was going to be a big dog. He did quite well there and when he "graduated," the school had a ceremony. He received a certificate wrapped around a dog biscuit and tied with a piece of yarn.

We played with him in the back yard and he just loved it. I bought him a little football which he chased frantically. He liked to rough-house with Ray. Later when I joined the New Mexico Mountain Club, I took him on hikes. When I was getting ready with my fanny pack and boots, he knew he was going and became very excited. On the trails, we did not have to keep him on a leash. He ran back and forth up ahead and back to me. One bright Sunday afternoon I met the group at a trailhead in the Sandias with Big Foot. One lady walked up to me and said, "I don't remember your name, but I remember Big Foot."

When he was about fourteen years old, I had to have the vet put him to sleep as he had arthritis in his back legs and could not get up anymore. I was devastated for a long time, and I still miss him. My vet just adored him, too, and suggested that I make a scrapbook about him which I did. Friends gave me a gift certificate to buy flowers for my yard in his memory. Other friends from the Mountain Club gave money in his memory to the Society for Prevention of Cruelty to Animals. I finally got another dog after about twelve years without one.

When Big Foot was about four years old, I adopted a beauti-

THE ISLETA PUEBLO ADVENTURE

ful, little black and white kitty. I taught Big Foot to leave the kitty alone, and eventually they became friends. I have a picture of them together on the floor of my den. I named the cat Kacey for K. C. or kitty cat. He was also quite loveable and loved to have his picture taken. Sometimes he watched TV and was very discriminate about his TV-HA! By the time he was about thirteen years old, his hearing had become bad. He liked to go out at night and come back in around midnight when I woke up. One night he didn't come back, not even the next morning. I was really worried. Then at lunch, the phone rang and some neighbor kids said they thought my cat was sick in the street. I ran out and he was dead over by the curb in front of a neighbor's house. I think he did not hear a car in the night and was hit. I had him cremated just as I did Big Foot, and I have both their ashes in cute containers.

I loved to teach Reading and Language to the Native American children. I quickly figured out that if they came to school speaking only their native tongue, they had to learn to read and write in English in order to succeed in all areas of learning.

When I went to Northern Arizona University in the 1960s, I wanted to get a Master's Degree in Teaching Reading. They did not offer it then. Later, in the 1970s, I decided to go to the University of Arizona in Tucson. The University of New Mexico did not offer such a degree at that time. Ray and I were thinking of moving to Oklahoma City where I hoped to get a job as a Reading Specialist.

I started attending the University of Arizona in the summer of 1976, continued during the summers of 1977 and 1978 and received the Master's in Teaching Reading, K-12 grades.

I loved Tucson and the beautiful palm-tree-lined boulevards

33

and campus streets. I stayed in the dormitory the first two summers; during the last one, I decided to treat myself to an apartment with a swimming pool. The only thing that I remember about the apartment was lying out by the pool one Saturday afternoon. I think that I really began an interest in nuclear development as I heard other people talking about a place that I had never heard of at the time: Hanford in the state of Washington. I have learned much more about it since, that there are huge problems with the storage of nuclear waste there and around the country.

3

North Texas Roots

Flashback to my roots in North Texas where I was born. The place is about fifty miles north of Dallas. This is not the wide-open spaces as in West Texas; it WAS beautiful country with rolling hills and green pastures dotted with furrowed rows of the black-land farms. Now, it is being developed quickly; I barely recognize where I grew up. The area has become part of the huge sprawl of the millions of people moving to the Dallas-Ft. Worth Metroplex.

Ted and Erma Walker, my parents, were share-croppers and never owned a square foot of land in their hard lives. My Mom worked right beside my Dad in the fields. I was one of seven children, three boys and four girls. My Mom once said that she had two families. Her first child, Hazel Rae, was followed quickly by three boys. I came along nine years later, as the beginning of the second family. I was followed by two younger sisters, Mary and Jo. I never saw the small shack where I was born, but Hazel gave me a picture of an old place that she said looked like it.

ANTELOPE RUNNING

The three boys, Bob, Dick and Jack, liked to tell the story about the June 1st day when I made my appearance. They said that they were shocking grain that day, and when they came home for lunch, there were cars parked in the front yard and they had a new baby sister. Shocking grain was a method used as the second step in harvesting grain. The oats or wheat were cut down with a binder. Then they were gathered by hand into bundles and tied with twine and left to stand in the field until they were later picked up. This method is not used any longer as the harvest is now done with machinery.

We moved several times and had three different landlords that I remember. From stories that I recall, they were not hard taskmasters; however Jack, my youngest brother, says we would not have had a place to live if it were not for the three sons who could pick a lot of cotton. Our first landlord was Mr. C. My first recollection of being invited out to lunch was when he and his wife had us up for Sunday "dinner," as we called it then. Mrs. C. was already elderly, and I am sure it was an effort for her to cook for extra people.

One of Mr. C's places was far off the highway, back in a field. We had to walk down the road to catch a bus for school. Sometimes, it was very muddy, but Jack would lead us "out." The people who lived in the house where we went to catch the bus later became part of the family. My sister, Mary, married their son. I do not believe the romance started in those early days, however.

Mary and I attended the small country school in the village of Cannon. It was a rather square, white-wood building with three rooms. One room housed first through fifth grades; another sixth, seventh and eighth. Across the back was a small gym. The only thing I remember about gym was trying to stand on my head up against the wall, which I could never do. There was no running water and so we used a little outhouse. I had my first exposure to the "f' word in the outhouse. It was carved in an easy-to-see space on the inside wall. I guess we drank from a dipper in a water bucket as we did at home.

I still remember learning to read from a little green, paper-back book about Dick and Jane. I took the book home at night and read aloud to all the family. We had no electricity then, and I learned to read by a coal-oil lamp. I was so proud of myself. I still really hate to smell coal-oil or diesel fuel. My Mom fixed our lunches. She made wonderful little individual chocolate pies for us. They consisted of a circular piece of pie dough with butter, sugar and cocoa sprinkled in one side and folded over; it was then baked in the oven. She also made delicious fried peach pies.

There were loving, family stories about my reading so loudly when I was just six years old in the first grade, and, how I came home from school with chocolate all over my face. Think I began my chocolate addiction back then. HA!!

I did not have music education in those days. The only music, at all, was a rhythm band. I always wanted to play the tambourine, but always got the rhythm sticks.

I do remember playing and singing a little children's song called "Skip to My Lou, My Darling" – Can't get a red bird, a blue bird will do, skip to my lou...." Later in high school, our speech teacher had a Christmas program. All I remember is our class singing, "Winter Wonderland" – Sleigh bells ring, are you listening..." We girls had to wear long, black, full skirts and white blouses. We also had a senior play where I was given a part – so fun!

North Texas received tons of rain during those years. One rainy Sunday afternoon, we had been down to visit an aunt and uncle. We had no car and so we walked, often through mud. When we got home, my brother Jack walked in the house in front of me. He wiped his feet on the "mudraker" by the steps and I said, "Jack, your feet are as muddy as Hell." I think I heard similar language from my uncle.

My mom heard me and said, "Your Dad is going to give you a whipping when he comes in." I ran in the house and hid under the bed. I had seen his belt and knew I did not want to feel it. He did not touch me, though. The only corporal punishment I remember came from my mom using a peach tree limb on my bare legs during the summer. There was a peach tree on the north side of the front yard, which was quite convenient for her. It is ironic that peaches are now one of my favorite fruits. Ha!

Those summers in North Texas during the 1940's were very hot weather, even at night. We begged our mother to let us sleep on pallets on the front porch. Sometimes she would permit it. She was not a very strict disciplinarian, although she did have high expectations for us. She was one of the old school parents. She taught us to be perfectly honest and instilled the value of hard work. She did this by example as she hoed cotton and worked in the field. When my brother, Dick returned from the Marine Corps in World War II, he had an old, heavy overcoat. I still remember a cold winter morning when my mother wore that old overcoat as she stood at the well where she drew water for the livestock and our use.

A dear friend of my early adult years later wrote in a book, which she gave me after my mother's death in 1983: "IN MEMORY OF YOUR MOM WHO LIVED HER LIFE FULLY AND COURGEOUSLY."

I worshipped my mother, although as a teen-ager I often yelled and we had many word "fights." I never felt that she loved me as I loved her. Later, in psychology classes in college, I learned about the "middle child." I was the fifth of seven children. I will never forget how she encouraged us in school and helped us with homework. I recall sitting at the old dining table doing some math problems which were frustrating me. She was washing dishes, and she dried her hands on her apron and came over and helped me. This is why I do not have a lot of patience today when parents give excuses for not helping children with their homework, or they do not stress education, i.e., the importance of regular attendance in school and doing homework. Also, the "putdowns" about school annoy me – that it is dull and boring. I told my little fourth and fifth graders that I was not doing a TV show. This was probably in the early 1980s.

My mother was a very intelligent woman. She had nearly finished high school when she was married at seventeen. She was an inspiration to me and much of what I later became was to make her proud of me. I remembered how proud she was of my three older brothers when one was captain of the football team and another was president of his senior class. Yet she never was able to see them play a game. I think my dad "bummed" a ride to town a few times to see Jack play football.

Mary, Jo and I, the younger children of our large family, did not have much contact with our grandparents. My paternal grandparents passed away before we were born or soon after. My mother's parents lived in Dallas, about fifty miles away. I remember going down to visit them only one time. Mama Smith, as she was called, was not a happy grandma. I never recall her baking cookies or doing fun things with us. The only things that I remember about going there were the milk bottles from the morning delivery on the back porch. Also, a horse-drawn vegetable wagon came down the street to sell produce.

Several years after my grandmother passed away, Papa Smith

came to stay with us. He was somewhat grouchy and complained of his lumbago. He spoke adamantly against all drinking. Even so, when the older brothers brought home a fifth of whiskey at Christmas, Papa Smith cleared his throat and said, "Maybe a little hot toddy would help my cold." We thought that he was hard of hearing, but my Mom always said that he hears what he wants to hear.

In my formative years during the 40's we lived on a farm in an area called Stringtown. The area consisted of a straight road for a mile or so where the houses and farms were "strung out" along the road. There were two families who lived south of us that I will never forget. One family had three children, two boys and a girl, and the other had only one boy. Those families became like relatives. One of the women came by and took my mom to the laundromat and to the grocery store regularly.

We spent time with the children constantly, every chance we had. We played touch football, basketball (one family had a goal) and baseball. We also played tin can down and hide and seek, the children's outdoor games of the time. In winter, our parents met with the other parents to play "Forty-two," a domino game similar to bridge, where you bid for tricks. We children gathered together at the kitchen table to play Monopoly or 500 Rummy.

On hot summer evenings, we played in "the pool." A rock pit had been dug to get rock for the Stringtown road which was usually very muddy. The rock pit made a great swimming pool for about one month at the beginning of the summer. Later it became stagnant, since there was no spring or outlet. I learned to swim there. Tommy, one of the Stringtown fathers, held his big farm hand under my tummy until I learned how to paddle on my own. We went down to the pool late in the evening when it was cooler.

I remember borrowing someone's ice cream freezer and making

ice cream on the back porch on a hot summer evening. On warm summer nights, we took our baths in a big number-three washtub on that back porch. One Sunday morning Mother came out on that porch to tell Mary and me that our new puppy had been run over while we were in town with the neighbors, Saturday night. Mother said we would not have cried any harder if she had been hit by a car.

When I was in fourth grade at the old country school called Cannon School, there was an old brown book with black-and-white one-half page pictures. One depicted either Venice or Vienna. At the time, I remember thinking that I'd love to visit there someday. Children should always have big dreams. As an adult, I traveled to both historic old cities.

Fourth grade class at Cannon Country School

I made my first friends in Stringtown. My dear Mickie became my best friend for years. She lived on a large farm with her many brothers and sisters. I loved to spend the night with her. Her mother was a big, round woman with an infectious laugh. She plaited my long auburn hair into French braids. Breakfasts at Mickie's house were unforgettable. Her mom served fried ham with red-eye gravy, as well as hot biscuits with white gravy. The brothers would throw biscuits up and down the table. I can still hear Mrs. Rigsby saying, "Now Raphael, stop that."

We also played in the hay loft of their big barn. Her brothers made a cart using boards and four wheels from an old cultivator. A cultivator is a type of plow. The boards were attached to the axles of the wheels. The boys fastened chains on the right and left front to guide it. We rode down the hill yelling and screaming. When Mickie spent the night with me, my mom played "Hide the Thimble" with us in the kitchen. Mickie still recalls this when I see her. I have a picture of our fourth-grade class, seven of us, at a school picnic in a nearby pasture. In those days we didn't have to have permission slips to leave school and walk down the road to a pasture. When I was nine years old, there was a revival at the little Cannon Country Church near the school. I joined the church and was baptized in a pond in that same pasture.

I went to Cannon School through the fifth grade. At that time Texas rolled out a program called consolidation of schools that included an extension from eleven grades to twelve. As part of the program, our little country school was closed and we went to school in town. I skipped sixth grade and went into seventh in the Van Alstyne system. All that I remember from that year was my Texas History course which was very boring – all we did was work in a workbook. In eighth grade most of the class still didn't know their multiplication tables. I remember Miss Muphree, the teacher, drilled on those facts with flash cards to catch us up. She always wore black suits. Later, I vowed that when I became a teacher, I would dress in bright colors.

During our graduation exercises from eighth grade, I was salutatorian of our class. I still have a yellowed, faded copy of my speech written by my English teacher, Mrs. Jay. The valedictorian was another Betty. She and I were friends all through high school.

Salutatory

Parents, Members of the School Board, Teachers, and Friends:

The Eighth Grade Class of 1945 bids you welcome. We have looked forward to this occasion with happy anticipation. Now, you are here to share this hour with us, and we are glad.

There was once a wise old man who knew much about human nature. He saw three young men passing his doorway.

To the first one who passed he said, "Young man, whom are you following?"

The young man replied, "I follow after pleasure."

The old man warned him to be cautious on his way.

The second young man answered to the same question, "I follow after riches."

The wise old man advised him

2

to beware of the dangers that would
befall him and told him to let
prudence be his guide.

To the youngest he said, "And
young man, whom do you seek?"

The youngest said, "I follow
after duty."

And each went on his way.

Years passed, and again the
old man came upon the three
wanderers.

"My good man", said he to the
first, "It was you who followed
after pleasure. Did you overtake
her?"

"No, father," he ~~replied~~, "pleasure
is but a phantom that that flies
as one approaches."

"You did not follow the right
way, my son. And you who sought
after riches how did you fare?"

"Riches is a sore burden. Pleasure
is not of it. I am distressed" he said.

"You did not follow the right

3

way, my son, ---- And "you", he
said, addressing the youngest.
"As I walked with duty, pleasure
and riches walked by my side
and my burdens were light."
"It is ever to use, said the wise
old man. "He who makes duty
his companion, makes companions
of three; pleasure, riches and duty.
Fellow-classmates, let us remember
this simple little story. Before
a duty before use. It is our business
to obtain an education within the
next few years. During these
formative years of our lives let
us resolve to equip ourselves
for a future of usefulness.
We want learning and we want
to know how to live with our
fellowman. As we train our minds
we want to build character.
"How empty learning, and
How vain is art,
Unless they mend the life
And guide the heart.

ANTELOPE RUNNING

High school was not a happy time for me. Today I would be called a nerd. I listened to my teachers and wanted to learn everything I could. The teachers were very kind and dedicated to their work. There was one, however, who was particularly important to me – my high school History/Speech teacher. She was quite dynamic with her flashing dark eyes and her passion for History. She used to quote the Declaration of Independence, saying "All men are created equal." She and my mother had a strong impact on me, helping to form my ideals regarding Negroes. There were quite a few in our little home town. They were required to live out at the edge of town and we had to go through their area in order to get into town. The sewer was near there and I hated that it was placed near their living area.

A black family lived down the road from one of the farms where we lived. One day L., the family's father came up to our house to borrow a cup of sugar. My grandfather who was living with us told him that he must come to the back door. My gracious mother told him later that he did NOT have to come to the back door. This was the beginning of the formation of my philosophy about other races. This experience proved invaluable many years later when I taught with wonderful black teachers. My mom's insistence that the black man could come to our front door proved an example of how parents influence a child's thinking. As the song from "South Pacific" says on this subject, "You have to be taught..."

One favorite recollection takes place at a farm where we had a couple of old cedar trees in the front yard. Mary and I were just little girls looking for something to do on a summer day. We decided to build a playhouse under the old trees. We found some old boards and some rocks and bricks to lay the boards across. Then we asked Mother for some jars or cans to put on the planks. This was our "kitchen." When we finished, we sat down and Mary said, "Now, Missus, what shall we talk about?" My answer was not very kind as I said something like, "I don't want to play anymore."

When I was about a sophomore in high school, my older brother, Dick was home from the University of Texas where he was going to pharmacy school. I was debating whether I should take Home Economics the next year in school. I will never forget him saying, "If you are going to college, you don't need that" So I took Algebra I and II and Chemistry instead in high school. These courses were so valuable, ten or twelve years later when I went to college to become a teacher, I took College Algebra and Trigonometry, since six hours of Math was required for my teaching certification. I attended a Liberal Arts College which had higher standards than state schools. Dick was the first person to ever mention college to me, but the idea was always in the back of my mind. Ten years after high school, it finally became a possibility.

In the late summer we had to pick cotton and help with the farm work. I still recall the last day we had to pick. I was a senior in high school at the time. I remember saying to myself as I held up the last boll before quitting time, "This is the last time that I will ever do this, unless I am very hungry." HA, HA! I could not have foreseen that in the not-too-distant future, machines were developed to pick the cotton.

Mother always saw to it that we went to school the first day it started after Labor Day. Some of my friends had to stay out and pick cotton until all the crop was in. I looked forward to going to town to buy my school supplies – a Big Chief red tablet and a new box of Crayolas. I always anticipated the beginning of

school. I seemed to sense when I was very young that this education was my ladder to climb out of poverty.

L. to R, Mary, my sister, Daddy, Betty

Some today speak of a "lost work ethic." It was ingrained

in us by my parents' hard work. That hard work was just a fact of life. They did not lecture us on this; it was just by their wonderful example. We just grew up believing that was the only way. My mother was such an inspiration to me as she always encouraged me. When I came home from school all upset about some bully harassing me, she would say, "Someday, you can get out of here." I believed her and looked forward to that time. Whatever I became, is largely because of her belief in me. I wanted to make good grades in school and be a successful adult to bring honor to the family.

Our last landlady was Mrs. Cannon who just loved my mother. When Mother was pregnant with Jo, the last child, Mrs. Cannon brought over milkshakes and chicken soup so that she would have a healthy diet. I learned to love her too, and many years later after I was married, my husband and I went by to see Mrs. Cannon on our way to visit my mom. Her husband, Jim, was a big rambunctious man who had attended the University of Texas. He claimed to have helped write the song, "The Eyes of Texas."

Mr. Cannon purchased a little John Deere tractor when Mary and I were about eight and ten years old. We both remember driving the tractor through the cornfield while our dad picked the corn and threw it in the wagon behind. We also did the driving when he was loading hay up on the wagon.

In 2006, on a trip to Grand Lake, Colorado, to visit friends who were working in Rocky Mountain National Park as volunteers, my sisters and I joined our friends on a drive up towards the top of the Mountain. We drove by an old fishing and hunting lodge that is now an historic site. Our friends said we should visit it during our stay. About the last day we were there, Jo, Mary and I went over to see it. On the way to the lodge, we crossed a stream that is the headwaters of the Colorado River. Near the lodge there were some pieces of old, rusty farm equipment. My sister, Jo, wanted to sit on the old hay rake exactly like we used to have when we farmed with the Cannons; I took her picture sitting on it as she remembered playing on it as a child.

One of my favorite memories is the year when I was nine years old. I recall a cloudy, cold November morning. Mary and I slept in a cold north side bedroom. There were cracks in the walls covered over with rose-flowered wallpaper. Our mom heated flatirons or bricks to put at the foot of our bed on cold winter nights. She wrapped them in pieces of old blanket that were nice and warm on our feet. I loved it when Mary "scooched" to my back. One morning I was awakened about dawn by voices and a lot of commotion going on in the front room where my mom and dad slept. I got up to see what was going on, but I was told to go back to bed. Turns out our old country doctor was there delivering my new baby sister, Jo. The blackland field just south of the house had been neatly plowed and I recall the lonely sound of mourning doves that gray, late, autumn morning.

Jo was a happy child. Maybe one reason was because our dad was so proud of her. He carried her around when we were all in town on Saturday night. He was about fifty years old when Jo was born.

My dad had one full brother, Uncle Vern and wife Aunt Mirtie. He was short and "tubby" and she was very tall and thin. They had their own unique personalities and did not fit any mold. When they came to visit us, Aunt Mirtie always wore a small, flat hat. When they left, she just plopped that old hat on her head without looking in any mirror. We thought that was so funny. My Mom said that she "ate like a bird" and took out one pea and cut it in half. They had no children and lived way up in a remote area northwest of us called Woodbine. They ran a general store that was fun to visit. Aunt Mirtie had an old-fashioned pump organ that she let me play. They gave me a lovely wristwatch when I graduated from high school—my first watch.

When I was in grade school and the teacher talked about eating your vegetables, I thought that was a good idea. Later, Uncle Vern and Aunt Mirtie gave us a big new International Harvester electric refrigerator. Before that we had an old fashioned ice box that had to have a fifty pound block of ice put in the top. The iceman "cometh" only in the summertime then. I remember I hated to empty the drain pan at the bottom.

So when Uncle Vern and Aunt Mirtie gave us the new electric frig, I was so proud of it. Mother talked about how I wiped it off to keep it clean. I have never wanted one of those old ice box models you now see as "antiques"—HA!

Another wonderful memory is about my youngest brother Jack who was about eight or nine years older than I. He is the only one of the older group of the siblings that I remember at home. The others left home after high school to go to Dallas or Houston to find work. I remember Jack walking home from school – about five miles – with his football jacket tied around his waist. He was either whistling or yodeling as he came home. He was kind to Mary and me and took us fishing in the creek down behind our house.

ANTELOPE RUNNING

We were never allowed to go with Jack again after Mary and I had a fight over who was going to hold the fishing pole. Jack went up to dig some more worms on the bank above. Mary had the pole, and I tried to grab it and she pushed me in the creek. I still remember going under – I thought for the third time – while the muddy water rushed over my head. I thought, "I guess this is it." Jack ran down to get me out, and then we had to go home. I was dripping wet and Jack told us that we would never go fishing with him again.—HA!!!

I also remember going rabbit hunting in the snow one winter with him. If he killed a rabbit, he took it home and skinned it. Then my mom fried it. The rabbit was very juicy with hot biscuits and white gravy. It tasted like the dark meat of chicken.

Jack married his high school sweetheart and they had four children – two girls and two boys. I remember them coming up to visit us on the farm. They also visited us for Christmas when Mother, Jo and I lived in Dallas on Ninth Street. We lived in a big old house with big trees in the front yard. I can still see the little boys, Mark and Tim, playing in the front yard kicking through the thick layer of dead leaves.

One of my favorite memories from childhood is my mom singing to us. I have no idea where she learned so many old songs as she had not heard a radio until the 1940's. She had a beautiful soprano voice and sang songs like "Red River Valley," "My Darling Clementine," "Isle of Capri," "Red Wing" and "Springtime in the Rockies." "Springtime in the Rockies" was one of my favorites. Many years later I spent so many happy days hiking in the Pecos Wilderness northeast of Santa Fe and in southern Colorado, both part of the southern Rockies. My younger sister Mary's favorite was "Isle of Capri" and mine was "Red Wing," a song about a little Indian maiden whose sweetheart went off to battle and never returned. Mother sang that and I would get big tears in my eyes. Isn't that ironic that many years later I became a teacher of "little Indian maidens and young braves."

In north Texas in 1930's and 40's, we often had ice and snow storms. When we had sufficient snow to pile up, we begged our mom to make snow ice cream. It is very simple: Just find some clean snow, high up, dip it in a large bowl, and add sugar and milk. It makes a nice treat.

When I was about fourteen, I began my life-long photography habit. One weekend morning, we woke to glistening trees frozen with ice. I grabbed the little Kodak Brownie box camera and took lovely pictures in the morning sunlight.

Erma Gwendolyn Smith Walker, my mother, was a beautiful brunette. She loved to tell the story about seeing a picture from a family reunion in South Carolina where she was born. She said there was an Indian woman in the back row, so she liked to believe that she was part Cherokee. She looked as if it were quite possible with her dark brown eyes, dark complexion and high cheek bones. My sister, Mary, and I "bugged" our mom to figure how many generations back the Indian woman lived. We figured out that we were 1/128 Cherokee – HA!

Erma G. Walker, my mother, at about 17-18

NORTH TEXAS ROOTS

When I was growing up on the farm, one of our favorite things to do was go to town on Saturday with our wonderful neighbors. Years earlier, when Mary and I were small, one couple where we lived had a Model A Ford, front seat with a rumble seat behind. Mary and I rode in it to town on warm Saturday nights. On Saturday afternoon we went to the movies where Roy Rogers or Gene Autrey was playing in a Western. Then we went to Trotters' to get a delicious hamburger made while you waited. The movie was probably a quarter and the burger about the same. After sundown, we met with our girlfriends from school and walked around and around the square hoping to see our latest boyfriend.

I remember one of my first heartthrobs was the cousin of one of my girlfriends. The main thing that I remember is he had quite a shock of very black hair in the front. The Carnival usually came to town every summer. I recall riding the Farris Wheel with Robert, and he gave me a little chalk squirrel that he had apparently won playing a game. While we walked around and around the square, our moms and dads stood around beside the cars visiting with friends and neighbors on the hot summer evenings.

4

World War Two

I wanted to write about World War II. I was nine years old when Pearl Harbor occurred, December 7, 1941.

That previous summer I remember my brother, Dick, was home from his job in Houston. The "war clouds" were looming even then, and I recall him saying, "For a nickel, I'd join the Navy." I remember jumping up and down and saying, "Don't anyone give him a nickel." He did join before the war started, and he and brother, Bob, were both in the Navy as pharmacist's mates. This would prove decisive. Later, they both chose pharmacy as a career, and went to the University of Texas on the G.I. Bill and became pharmacists. Jack, the youngest of the three brothers, was in the Army Air Force, before the Air Force became a separate branch of the military.

Jack never went overseas, since he already had started a family. His job was in radio and communications. That fits. I remember him making a crystal radio set with copper wire and an oatmeal box when he was young, and at home. I recall him getting static on it, but I don't remember voices.

Photo by Susan Barton

MCKNIGHT'S MEDICINES — Toni Tillett, right, watches as pharmacist Bob Walker chooses from an array of hundreds of modern medicines. : Dependable prescription service is one of the reasons McKnight Drug serves so many Garland residents. Garland's oldest drug store location, the historic facility, housed in the old Masonic Building, was among the first brick structures to be built on Garland's downtown square at the turn of th century. McKnight Drug's site has been occupied continuously by a drugstore for more than 60 years.

Bob Walker, my brother, in his Pharmacy

Dick was in the Solomon Islands on Bougainville, in the jungles. We sent him cookies, and he told my mom to send them in coffee cans, since they had rats over there as big as cats. One day we went to the little country store to get some sugar to make cookies. Big rolls of barbed wire were sitting by the door on the porch of the store. I was so excited to buy ingredients for Dick's cookies that I ran by the wire too fast and tore cuts in my leg. It must have been summer, since I was wearing shorts. I still have the scars just above my left knee.

Our family was certainly involved in WWII, and we were quite patriotic. Our Mother taught Jo, the youngest sister, to sing the "Marines' Hymn." She stood on an old kitchen chair and sang "From the halls of Montezuma to the shores of Tripoli...." I am sure we all clapped and told her how good she was. This was most likely done after a Thanksgiving or Christmas Dinner. I just loved it when my older brothers and sisters came home for the holidays. We could not afford a turkey, but my mom fixed a big, juicy hen with cornbread dressing and cranberries. Those were unforgettable family times.

Bob was on a landing craft, LST 686, when they went back to the Philippines, and landed at Leyte Gulf. He never said much about the War until the last few years of his life. I became interested in geography and the world, and wanted to locate the places on the map where they were all stationed. Jack's wife, Jacqueline, gave me a scrapbook and I cut out clippings of military leaders from the newspaper that our landlord gave us. I put them in my scrapbook along with pictures of "the boys" as my mom called them. I still have the scrapbook. It's in my large safe deposit box at the bank. Jacqueline was such a sweet sister-in-law. She gave us a magazine called "Song Hits." It contained the most popular songs of the day, which were played on the radio program, "The Hit Parade." She also gave me my first camera, a little Kodak Brownie box camera.

Speaking of the radio, there is a great story about how we

got our first radio. One of Dick's buddies in the Navy was a guy named Art Gaunt from Providence, Rhode Island. He asked my dad to buy him a calf and raise it on our farm so that he could say that he had cattle in Texas. My dad complied, and when it was time to sell the calf, Art asked us to keep the money for a radio. My favorite program was "The Lone Ranger," which came on each week night at 6:30. We also listened to Jack Benny, Fred and Gracie Allen and Edgar Bergen with Charlie McCarthy. In the summer, we listened to the soap operas. The only one I remember was "Stella Dallas."

For such a young girl, I took the war very seriously. I naively thought, when this is over, we will have peace. Before Pearl Harbor when I was only about six or seven, in 1938 or 1939, I heard Mother and Daddy in the kitchen talking about Hitler. I had never seen a policeman, but I guess I had heard about them in first grade in school and so, I said, "Why can't the policemen stop him?" Years later came Hiroshima and Nagasaki. I was in high school at that time, and I just didn't know what to think of such a horror. What about my future in such a world?

I recall that our dad thought highly of Roosevelt, and logically so, since some of the "New Deal" programs probably helped us survive. Dad worked on the WPA, the Works Projects (or Progress) Administration. We also received surplus food from one of those programs. Mom never liked the whole wheat or "brown flour" as she called it. We had a garden for several years in the "40's. It was lovely garden located down through the pasture, across the "branch" or stream in a shady spot.

We grew Irish potatoes, green beans, corn, tomatoes, okra, yellow and white squash, and cucumbers. I hated to pick the okra, since it had stickers. I was always glad when it was too small to gather. My youngest sister, Jo, who was born in 1940, always liked to go down to the "gardie." Mother worked very hard during the summer canning those vegetables. I remember the tall quart jars of green beans. The job she dreaded the most was canning corn, since scraping it off the cob was a very messy job. Speaking of food, I remember the little ration books for sugar and other staples.

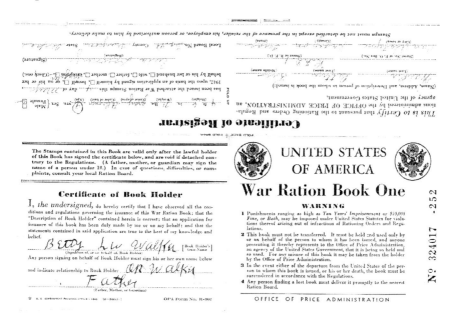

I had one older sister, Hazel Rae, who was the oldest child of the family, fifteen years older than I. She lived with our grandmother in town. She graduated from high school when I was two years old and went to Dallas to work. Courses such as typing and shorthand were not offered then, so she wasn't prepared for a job. She went to work as a nanny for the rich. I recall the story years later that she worked for Tom Clark, so she must have taken care of Ramsey. After that she worked for the owners of English Freight Company. She took care of two little girls who were about the same age as my younger sister, Mary and I. When those girls tired of their nice clothes – after wearing them just a few times – Hazel brought them to Mary and me. Before the war, she met and married a handsome "Okie" who was working in Dallas. They came to visit us on the farm. Hazel was a beauty, and I remember her purple wool suit. I wanted to be like her when I grew up, so I learned to love beautiful clothes and nice things.

Her husband's name was Cecil. He was good to us like a brother. Once, Hazel and Cecil found a mother dog beside the road on a trip up from Dallas. She had eleven puppies. Mary and I were able to keep one. Hazel gave Mary and me little toy suitcases one Christmas. Mine was blue and Mary's was red. The new puppy chewed on the corner of mine, which was very upsetting.

In WWII, Cecil joined the famous 36th Division in the Texas National Guard. He first went to North Africa and helped drive out the German general, Rommel. Then they went to Italy and were part of the landing at Salerno Beach. The Division advanced much further north and the soldiers were almost caught in the Battle of the Bulge, where the Germans had Americans surrounded. I loved to get his "V-Mail" letters to us. My sister, Jo, has a beautiful small picture of the Cologne Cathedral that he sent us.

I must have written letters to Bob and Dick. Some of my treasures are letters I received from each of them for my birthday. In the letters they recalled what they were doing on June 1, 1932, the day I was born.

South Pacific
June 11, 1944

Dear Betty Lu,

Your letter of May 31st came today — was very glad to Hear from you.

I was thinking of you on your birthday — I remember well twelve years ago. Bob, Jack, Hazel, and I were tickled pink when we found we had a baby sister. I remember us teaching you to walk (we thought you never would) you first said Bobo — I believe it was your first word. I use to help mother with you — sing to you, rock you, and walk you to keep you from crying; however, you cried but little. Then you were very sick with pneumonia — the doctor was doubtful, and we were all worried very much. I was living at Unkie's then — but they came for me and I stayed until you were almost well again — Then little mary came and joined us at that time — she was very tiny, but

-2-

strong from the first. I remember well when you first started to school — smart as a whip, a little on the timid side, but able to take care of yourself. You've come a long way in these twelve years and I'm very proud of you — you are getting to be quite a big young lady now — yes I remember twelve years ago very well, just keep as you are now for the next twelve years and there after and you will always be on the right course.

Unfortunately I can't send you a grass skirt now. The natives on this island don't wear them as far as I know. I'll bring you a much better souvineer when I come — a grass skirt wouldn't last through the years anyway.

Congratulations on being exempt in all your final examinations at school.

I'm sure you and Mary are having a lot of good times in the "Camp-Fire Girls", am glad.

Hope you both had a good time in Dallas — and that Hazel

at sea
June 28, 1945.

Dear Beth:

I will write you a few lines & don't get
excited if you find it hard to read as
we are underway & that causes the table
to "shimmy" and make my writing look
as if I had a case of the jitters. But
I am OK except for my often mentioned
heat rash, & it is a bit better (I think).

I got your letter with the snap
shot enclosed & if that picture looks
like you, I wouldn't have known you
if I had met you on the street.
But I guess you have grown up
quite a bit since I saw you. It
is been almost two years now.

Congratulations on being
Salutatorian of your class, I took the
same position when I graduated from
Grammar school (ask mother) Of Course
I didn't have so much competition

In numbers as you did, but after all there are only six or eight in the running any way. I think mother still has my diploma etc, that is if she hasn't given it to Wilma. By the way I had to break out the "Webster" to find out how to spell "Salutatorian." I hear Mary did rather well in her studies also. I guess I was about the "dumbest" one in the family, oh well there has to be a family "blockhead" & it might have been you if it hadn't been me.

We have a basketball team & court on the back block. We have won 8 & lost ~~5, out last seven wins in a row.~~ I hurt my leg & was out for about 10 days but have got to start the last two games.

Well Betty I will close for now write again soon

love
Bob

WORLD WAR TWO

I still just love to read maps. I liked history in high school and college, although I only took the required hours. I would like to study more history some day. I am still interested in world affairs and one of my favorite things to do is to travel and see as much of the world as possible. I have been blessed to travel quite a lot and have been to eighteen foreign countries.

One wonderful outcome of travel is the interesting people I have met: tour guides who were with us for six weeks on a European college trip, another very bright young man in Costa Rica, a salesman at a Kiosk where I was trying to choose a tape of music. He suggested one by a group called "Editus." He said, "I think you will like this." He was so right, as it has become my favorite! The music is quite international. I have almost worn it out playing Rodrigo's "Aranjuez." It is very soft and lovely as it is Spanish classical guitar.

5

Leaving Home

May 28, 1949, I received that long awaited high school diploma. The summer before I graduated, I was in Dallas visiting relatives. I knew that I would be looking for a job the following May when I graduated. I looked through the ads of a Dallas newspaper just to get an idea of what was available. One ad by the City of Dallas caught my eye. It required the applicant to take a Civil Service Test to work for the City. I caught a bus and went down to City Hall and took the test. I did not hear anything about the test results, and thought that I had not made a passing grade. Well, this is an example of how slowly the wheels of government turn.

The following April before I was to graduate in May, I received notification from the City of Dallas that I should come in for an interview if I were still interested in the job. I was so excited when I went down for the meeting. I explained that I could not come to work until I graduated at the end of May. At that time, my High School in Van Alstyne, Texas, had exemption from finals if you had an A average. I was getting A's so, I went to work on May 23, one week before graduation. I traveled back to attend the graduation ceremony on May 28, 1949. My career was launched.

My position was as general clerk in the Office of the Building Inspector. Dallas was booming at this time after World War II. My job was to record all building permits in a big ledger-type journal. This included construction, electrical and plumbing permits. At the end of the month, I had to total all those permits by category and submit a report to the United States Department of Labor. I still remember the light blue paper on which it was printed. At lunch I relieved on the switchboard or took dictation from the bosses while their employees were out to lunch.

The head of the Department was a kindly, old gentleman who reminded me of Benjamin Franklin as he was somewhat short and stocky and wore square-lens glasses. He liked to talk about opera as I sat across from his old-fashioned desk.

In retrospect, I do not believe that there could have been a better place for an inexperienced, young girl just out of a small town high school to begin adult life. The people were just wonderful to me. It was a large office with about eighty people, mostly men who were the various kinds of inspectors. When I go back to Dallas now, I recognize some of the streets that were being developed with housing projects when I worked there.

Several of the men liked to tease me, and I made some of my first friends out of high school there. Most were perfect gentlemen and I rode to work with them. Only one or two got out of line, but nothing bad happened. I enjoyed going out to lunch and one lady and I became lifelong friends. She had such a positive attitude and laughed a lot.

One day we were going out to lunch and I forgot my gloves

(these were the "days" when we dressed up more – no jeans to work). Evelyn said, "You never know what you'll meet when you haven't got your gun." She was reared Quaker, and I never heard her criticize anyone.

We had women's softball team where I played. We also had a group who went square-dancing on Friday nights. This was such a different world from today, and I am sorry that youth now do not have access to such experiences. At this time I lived at the YWCA on North Haskell near Baylor Hospital. It was a nice clean place for young women to live. They served two meals a day, breakfast and dinner. We had to be in by 12:00 p.m. during the week and 1:00 a.m. on Saturday night.

In the beginning months on weekends, I caught a bus back to my home north of Dallas.

One Sunday evening when I returned to my room at the "Y," I had a roommate. I still remember she was sitting up against the wall on her bed reading a book. She did not talk much, but we became good friends. We had a lot in common as she grew up on a farm in northeast Texas, near a small community called Blossom.

We had wonderful times going to the YMCA in downtown Dallas for Friday night dances. We met boyfriends there and double-dated all around town. I remember once we went ice-skating. I have never been well-coordinated, and I fell down. Marlene's boyfriend, Ronnie, ran over my little fingernail. It was not serious, but we never went ice-skating again.

This living arrangement lasted a little over a year. Marlene had a sister named Barbara who was married to Max, a Marine stationed there at a Naval Air Base. The four of us decided to get an apartment. A new development in southwest Dallas called Wynnewood Village was our choice. We were all near the same age and had such wonderful times together, cooking and sharing.

One Sunday evening, the radio was on, and there was an important announcement. It said that the government needed secretaries in Washington, D.C. This was during the Korean War. The instructions said those interested in the job should go to their local post office and take the Civil Service Test for Secretary. I had made several friends at the "Y" and a steady boyfriend. However, Marlene and I decided that we wanted to do something different for our jobs.

We both went down and took the test. I failed the shorthand the first time, but they said that I could take it again in six months. I went to night school at the old Crozier Tech Vocational School and took a review course in shorthand. I passed this time, and in May 1951, Marlene and I were on our way to DC via a Trailways bus.

Before I was approved, the FBI did an investigation at my little high school in Van Alstyne. It was pretty exciting as they came and talked to my teachers. My mother said that the whole town was talking about it. Marlene had worked for the phone company as a secretary in Dallas. She knew someone in her office who knew a woman in DC. This lady had a row house there with an apartment upstairs that she wanted to rent. I still remember the address, 1642 Argonne Place, NW.

This was an adventure of a lifetime for two young women from Texas. I think we went sight-seeing every weekend for months. We saw all the usual sights the tourists visit: Mt. Vernon, The White House, and Capitol Building, Washington Monument, the Jefferson and Lincoln Memorials, Connecticut Avenue and other points of interest. One lovely Saturday morning, the two of us rented bikes and rode around the Tidal Basin (like a lake) near the Jefferson Memorial. We went to Hogates, a large seafood restaurant down by the wharf. We also went to a very nice restaurant called O'Donnells in the old Willard Hotel in downtown D.C. The waiters were all nice-looking young men dressed in black with little white towels over their arms. Ever since then, I have always liked to have men waiters at nice restaurants.

Marlene and I went to Friday night dances at the YMCA just as we had in Dallas. I love to remember dancing to Tommy Dorsey and Glenn Miller orchestras and meeting the new guys that were stationed near there. I met a tall Indian from Oklahoma that I thought was "the love of my life." His name was Al, and he introduced me to Jazz. It was called Progressive Jazz with stars like Dave Brubeck and George Shearing. We wanted to go the Clubs to hear them, but neither of us could afford that. Al was in the Air Force at Bolling Field, near the Anacostia Naval Base. He was in the Drum and Bugle Corps and marched in parades.

When Eisenhower was inaugurated in 1952, Marlene and I went and sat along the curb on Pennsylvania Avenue. Of course, I was watching for Al to march by just as much as I was for the limousine with the new president.

Another exciting thing that we did was to take a trip to New York City. I had wanted to see a Broadway show since I was a teenager. I had listened to an outstanding radio station in Dallas that played show music, semi-classical and classical. We bought tickets to "Wish You Were Here" – "They're not painting the sky as blue this year Wish you were here..." We made hotel reservations at the Warwick Hotel (no longer there) and had a fantastic time seeing the sights. We were in Times Square on Halloween Night, 1951 or '52.

ANTELOPE RUNNING

In DC, another fun event in April (probably 1952) was the Cherry Blossom Festival. The cherry trees had been given to the United States by Japan many years before as a token of friendship. They were planted down by the Jefferson Memorial and the Tidal Basin. The Jefferson was my favorite Memorial with the classic Greek architecture. The cherry blossoms were so gorgeous with their pink flowers along the shore.

Sam Rayburn was my representative from north Texas. I called his office and he invited me to come down and visit him. I used some of my annual leave time and went down to the House Office Building to see him. He gave me a pass to attend a session of the House of Representatives. I went in and sat in the balcony. I don't remember what issue was discussed. I was also invited to a dinner at the Mayflower Hotel. I can't remember if that came from Sam Rayburn's office. The only thing that I remember is trying to observe other people so I would know which fork to use next.

Marlene and I worked in the same large office with rows of secretarial desks and the bosses' desks behind us. It was the Office of Price Stabilization which was a reincarnation of the old Office of Price Administration (OPA) of World War II.

Marlene met "the love of her life" at one of the Friday night dances. He was a tall, handsome, blonde, Nebraskan, and they made a striking couple, since she was tall and dark. When he shipped out to Wiesbaden, Germany with the Air Force, he didn't want her to stay in D.C. around all those guys. She went back to Dallas to wait for him.

I stayed in D.C., but I couldn't afford the apartment by myself. I found another nice place to live at the Young Women's Christian Home over on 2nd Street near the Capitol. I made new friends there and, on Sunday evenings, we went to concerts on the Capitol lawn. The military bands played there, and we saw Eddie Fisher with the Army Band one evening. I still remember him in his uniform.

By this time the OPS where I worked had been abolished, and I transferred to the Pentagon as a file clerk. It was quite boring, although I was cleared for "TOP SECRET." I didn't like my boss. He was a little lieutenant who seemed bored, too. The most interesting thing about the place was that there was another red head who was a secretary to a colonel. They found it necessary to attend meetings in Paris, at government expense I am sure. I remember the Department name but will not tell to protect the guilty.

I returned to Dallas in time to attend Marlene and Lee's wedding as a bridesmaid in October of 1953. I shared an apartment near Inwood Road where Marlene had lived before. It was not a great time in my life as I could not find a good job. After jumping around to different jobs, I finally landed a nice position at the Cotton Exchange Building. I worked as a secretary for a futures broker where a girlfriend that I knew in Dallas years before had worked. She had married and lived in a suburb called Garland. They were having a baby and she asked if I would like her job. Rek, my boss, was kind to me and liked to think that he taught me how to be a secretary, although I had already been one in D.C.

One year there was a big Ball at the Hilton Hotel celebrating the cotton industry. Rek found me a date with a tall German young man who was at the company learning the cotton business. I bought a beautiful mauve, ballerina-length evening dress and had a wonderful evening dancing to music from "My Fair Lady." I remember "I Could Have Danced All Night. . . ."

ANTELOPE RUNNING

After a couple of years there, my boss was getting out of the brokerage business. He found me a wonderful job with a cotton-exporting company in the same building. This was my best job yet, with Esteve Brothers and Company. They had offices all over the world. I sometimes spoke on the phone with Osaka, Japan, Sao Paulo, Brazil or Liverpool, England. Sometimes I answered the teletype machine if Madeline, the main secretary, was unavailable. I knew to jump up and answer if a little bell rang softly indicating a message was coming in from some faraway place.

Esteve Brothers Cotton Exporting Company was my favorite job as a secretary. The Company had been organized by a family from the Barcelona, Spain area many years before, I believe in the late 1890's. When I was there in the late 1950's it was headed by the senior Mr. Ramon Esteve. He was a kindly old gentleman; one evening he and his wife invited me to dinner at their gorgeous, big home in University Park, an exclusive area in Dallas. There were several sons who worked for the company, one in Mexico, another one in Sao Paulo. Brazil. I worked for one in Dallas.

I also acted as receptionist at the front desk. To the right and off to the side of me, sat Madeline Crocker, the secretary to the senior Mr. Esteve. She was another very kind, gentle soul, "of the old school" in mannerisms. We went to lunch on occasion when she was not too busy.

Before I went to work there in May of 1957, a girlfriend and I had planned to take a vacation to Mexico City and Acapulco in August. Since I had only been in the office a short time, I really hesitated to ask for eleven days off for a vacation three months later. One day when Madeline and I went to lunch, I told her about our plans. She said that she was sure that it would be alright, but she would check for me. She told me a few days later that it was fine. I was so happy and could not believe it.

Another very nice event: One July 4, the company was having a party on their cabin cruiser out on a lake near Dallas. They invited me to go, and this was another adventure for a young girl who had not been on a boat very much.

I had always wanted my life to be an adventure. I think that it really has been just that. With all the places I have been and the people that became my friends, I now believe that God was blessing me and guiding me all the way. I am thankful for it!!!! I will always remember the wonderful people who gave so much to me. I cannot express my feeling adequately.

I had the idea of attending college soon after high school graduation. Attached is a letter that I wrote to a government agency, re: loans to attend college.

ANTELOPE RUNNING

FEDERAL SECURITY AGENCY
OFFICE OF EDUCATION
WASHINGTON 25, D. C.

September 7, 1950

Miss Betty Walker
1206 North Haskell Avenue
Dallas, Texas

Dear Miss Walker:

Your letter of August 11 addressed to the Department of Labor
has been referred to this Office for reply.

We regret to inform you that at present there is no Federal
program of financial aid for non-veteran college students, either
in the form of scholarships, fellowships or loans, except in the
limited fields noted on the enclosed statement on "Financial
Assistance for Civilian College Students." A bill to provide for
a National program of scholarships was introduced in this session
of Congress but we cannot predict what action will be taken by the
Congress.

You may wish to consult the references listed below if they
are available in one of your local public or institutional libraries:

Federal Security Agency, Office of Education. Working Your
Way Through College and Other Means of Providing for College Expenses,
by Walter J. Greenleaf. Washington, D. C.: U. S. Government Printing
Office, 1940. 175 p. (Vocational Division Bulletin 210, 1940).

S. Norman Feingold. Scholarships, Fellowships and Loans.
Boston, Mass.: Bellman Publishing Company, Inc., 1949.

Clarence E. Lovejoy. Complete Guide to American Colleges and
Universities, "Scholarships for the Asking, and Loans, Too." New
York: Simon and Schuster, 1948.

If we can be of any further assistance, please feel free to
call on us.

Sincerely yours,

John Dale Russell, Director
Division of Higher Education

Enclosures

80

6

My Mid-Twenties and Beyond

In my mid-twenties and during the mid-1950s, I was living in Dallas, dating and dancing and having a great time.

My dad died in the spring of 1954. That summer I told my mom that she could move to Dallas, and we could share a home. She and Jo, the youngest child who was thirteen, moved soon after. It was a huge adjustment for both of them.

I attended Church at Oak Cliff Methodist and went to a Young Adult Group there. We had various social activities. I will never forget attending a wiener roast, a common social activity for young people at that time. I went over to the campfire to have another "dog." There sitting by the fire with a stick in his hand was this handsome guy with dark hair and dark eyes. He seemed friendly and we started talking. I could tell right away that he was a kind, gentle man and I certainly liked his great, dark face. We began dating after that.

About that same time, probably the Spring of 1959, I went to a Young Adult Retreat with the Church group up to a Methodist Church in Denton, Texas, about forty miles northwest of Dallas (at that time—not now, because Dallas has grown so much). The theme of the talk that Saturday evening was "Our Faith, Our Vocation, Our Mission,"

It really struck a chord with me as office work had become quite tedious to me.

After the service that Saturday night at the retreat, I went up to talk with the speaker. I still remember his name, Bill Weir. He was quite encouraging and told me about a lady that I should talk to. She was from the New York Office of the United Methodist Church, the Board of Missions. She happened to be at Southern Methodist University (SMU) in Dallas that weekend. He gave me a phone number where I could probably reach her.

When I was back home in Dallas the following Sunday afternoon, kinda tired, resting in the den, I said to myself, "You must get up and call that lady or you will be sorry for the rest of your life." I really feel God was talking to me at that time as He worked in all the events of my life. The lady advised me that I wouldn't want to go to SMU as it was too expensive – which I knew. She gave me the name of the Dean of Women at McMurry College in Abilene, Texas.

Her name was Mrs. Chappelle and I can never forget her. I called her the next week and we began to make plans for me to attend McMurry. I had a total of $500.00 in the bank at that time. She said she would help me find a part-time job and told me about some scholarships and government loans I could probably get. In the fall of 1959, I enrolled as a freshman at age 27 at McMurry College, now McMurry University. It was – and still is – a small school, around 1,300 enrollment. Mrs. Chappelle told me, "I'm going to find you a job off campus since you have previous office experience where you can make $1.00 an hour; we only pay $.50 and hour on campus."

She found me a job at a small children's clothing factory where I recorded sales in a ledger book. I was always so fortunate to get all my required classes scheduled in the morning. I went to the college cafeteria to eat lunch. Then I'd catch a little, rickety bus to the clothing factory. I got off at five, went back to campus, had supper – as we called it then – and then hit the books. I usually carried fifteen to sixteen credit hours every semester.

My professors were wonderful. I had graduated from a small town high school and had been out ten years. My English professor, Dr. Huff, was very kind as was my college algebra and trigonometry teacher, Ms Tate. In English class, during my second freshman semester, we had to write a term paper, using note cards, footnotes and a bibliography of at least fifteen sources. I was mortified as the only report I had ever written in high school was using the World Book Encyclopedia—HA! Both instructors told me, "If you have any problems, come by my office after 3:00 p.m." I really took them up on their offers.

Another wonderful "prof" was my Bible instructor. He was an older man and liked me, I believe. I met his wife and they invited me to a symphony orchestra concert – my first. I was so grateful.

The handsome, dark-eyed man that I met by the wiener roast campfire came to visit me on weekends at school. He still lived and worked in Dallas. Then, he applied for and obtained a job with the IRS in San Francisco as he was an accountant, a graduate from the University of Oklahoma. I went to College year-round and finished in three years plus one summer semester. When I finished, we planned to be married and live in California. But the "best laid plans of mice, men *and* women" often do not materialize.

During my third year in College, I stopped getting letters from

San Francisco. I was, of course, most upset, but I carried on. I went to live with my sister, Jo, and her husband in Oklahoma City during the summer of 1961 and went to Oklahoma City University and took six hours. Then, I went back to McMurry that fall and finished up the following summer.

I did not hear from "handsome" for six years. One birthday I received a bottle of Chanel Number 5. But I was so upset, I did not reply with a "thank you" note. I was working at Crownpoint Boarding School then, probably 1966. I had friend there, a buxom, Black teacher. I told her about the Chanel No. 5. In her wise manner, she said, "Walker, (my last name at that time), you better write that boy and thank him." I followed her advice and wrote him at the last address that I had in San Francisco. He had moved to Los Angeles, then back to his home in McAlester, Oklahoma. I will never again complain about the mail service as my letter followed him from all those places and to McAlester.

One dreary, winter evening after work, I went to the post office in Crownpoint as we had no home delivery. I was so ecstatic to find one of those long, funny cards from Ray. My thank you note had caught up with him. I called him that evening and we arranged to meet at the Ramada Inn in Amarillo, Texas, on Washington's Birthday weekend, 1967.

He brought me a beautiful set of candles (I still have them somewhere) and we decided to be married the following summer.

I asked for a transfer from Crownpoint to Tohatchi which was only twenty eight miles north of Gallup, New Mexico, where we hoped that he could get a job. We were married in Albuquerque at Trinity United Methodist Church on July 15, 1967. Ray was blessed to get a job at St. Mary's Hospital (later, McKinley General) in Gallup as the controller. We had a nice new home up on the hill at Chuska Boarding School at Tohatchi. It had a picture window in the front where we could see the Chuska Mountains to the West, near the New Mexico and Arizona border.

ANTELOPE RUNNING

We had wonderful friends, other couples and singles that I worked with at the school. We had them over for dinner and I remember making Mexican food – tacos, enchiladas and chili con queso. Ray liked to make the queso and considered himself a guacamole expert. A group of these same friends went across the mountains to Canyon de Chelly on a memorable weekend. We hiked down to the White House Ruins, an ancient Anasazi site dating back to 1100 A.D. that was the only trail at that time that could be hiked down.

On another trip with L., a boys' dormitory supervisor, the car climbed up the mountain to the home of a student who had run away from school. L. found him safe and sound with his parents. I will never forget that drive on the winding mountain road in the moonlight with snow glistening on the tall ponderosa pines. It was not even cold and a soft breeze was almost musical through the pines.

Another remarkable experience was going with L. through the mountains to a Yei Be Chai Dance. This is a Navajo ceremony that is held to heal the sick; I remember the dancers around the campfire. The ill person was in a hogan, where the medicine man prayed with him/her. Some of the most beautiful, expensive Navajo rugs come from the Yei Be Chai. They're known for their intricate designs and colors depicting the tall, thin dancers. My friends and I were also invited to another native dance at Crownpoint. It was a Fire Dance and was quite mystical. We sat around in a large circle made of juniper boughs with the fire in the center. The male dancers were naked to the waist with their bodies covered with white paint. It was hard to believe I was in the United States.

During my first year at Tohatchi, I taught at the Demonstration School up on the mesa called Chuska Boarding School. The school was established to train teachers from all over the Reservation to teach English as a Second Language. I was a second grade teacher as I had been my first year in 1962. As many as fifteen teachers or supervisors could enter my classroom through a back door at any time during the day, so I had to be very explicitly prepared every day with what "bosses" called narrative lesson plans. We had to know exactly everything we were going to say all day long. It was quite stressful and not a great way to begin the first year of a marriage.

I stayed there one year before transferring down the hill to the old Tohatchi Boarding School. There I taught sixth, seventh and eighth grade English. I didn't think I would like teaching the older children, but I came to enjoy the change and the challenge. Years before, children had been kept out of school to herd sheep, and I had boys who were fourteen and fifteen years old in my eighth grade class. They were tall and nice looking young men – most quite shy and polite. I asked a couple of them to draw me a picture of Monument Valley, a spectacular desert area way out in the western part of the Reservation.

The Valley is famous as a location for western films because of the huge volcanic plugs that stand like huge monuments to long forgotten heroes. Franklin and Thompson drew me a striking picture of the valley in pastel colors; it was about eighteen by twenty four inches. It is framed and hangs in the entryway to my home as another of my prized possessions. Many of the Native American children, especially boys, have an inborn artistic talent – never having had an art lesson. The girls do too. They grow up to weave the intricate designs in their rugs – designs entirely in their heads.

ANTELOPE RUNNING

My last year at Tohatchi Boarding School was in late 1960's. Another teacher and I, a wonderful man, Bob C., decided to take the eighth grade class to Phoenix for their graduation trip. We made reservations to stay at a motel with a pool as most of those children had never been swimming. We also planned to take them to the Heard Museum, which is famous for its collection of history and art of Southwest Indian cultures. Just south of Flagstaff I became very ill and was incapacitated for most of the trip. I had always wanted to go to the Heard and was looking forward to a relaxing swim, but the only thing I could do to help Bob C. was check on the girls to be sure that they were all in their rooms at the end of the day.

A Night on Mount Taylor

Mt. Taylor is an 11,000 feet plus volcanic mountain in western New Mexico near the town of Grants, just north of I-40. When Ray and I lived at Tohatchi, north of Gallup, one Sunday afternoon after church in Gallup, I talked Ray into driving up to the top of this peak. I had heard stories about how beautiful it was. It was around the first of April, and there was still snow at the higher elevations. We drove east on I-40 and found the exit up to a village of San Mateo and the Mountain. We went past the Village and were gradually climbing.

After a few miles we began to encounter more snow and puddles on the dirt road. Ray was a cautious individual and wanted to turn around. I remember saying, "Where is your spirit of adventure?" We kept going and, then, there was a larger puddle in the road. We were not in a four-wheel drive vehicle, but a Chevy Malibu. The car became stuck in the mud. No one believes this as it sounds like an Irish folktale, but there was a shovel right beside the road. Ray tried to dig under the back wheels, and I turned the engine on and tried to move the car forward with Ray pushing in the back. The back wheels just mired deeper into the thick mud. We both gathered up ponderosa pine branches and put under the back tires, and I tried the same procedure. This all went on for hours until it became dark and very cold.

We had to get inside the car and turn the heater on. I had learned after years "on the Reservation" to always carry a blanket in the car. We took it out of the trunk and tried to keep warm while, alternately, turning the heater on and off. This all happened a few days after Martin Luther King had been assassinated, and the murderer had not been caught. In my wild imagination, I figured he was hiding up on that remote mountain, and was going to tap on my window, and demand the car. He could not have gone anywhere if he had.

Daylight finally came, and the ground was so frozen, we just pulled right out. We finally reached Grants and a cafe. We trudged in there so muddy and dirty where I called my supervisor at Chuska Boarding School in Tohatchi, and said that I would not be in that day. I was never so glad to have some hot coffee and breakfast in all my life.

7

Living Life to the Fullest

In my twenties, I began a lifelong habit of having parties. It began when I was working as a secretary for the wonderful company, Esteve Brothers, in Dallas. I had my first party for Christmas in 1957 or 1958. I invited my boss, E., and he came with his brother G.

I was so excited and flattered. I remember fixing a grapefruit with toothpicks with cheese cubes stuck on the ends. I will never forget my dear friend, Evelyn, who brought bourbon balls with the recipe for them written on a large piece of white poster board. We stood it up on a chair for everyone to see. She also brought a hand-made gift. It was a "pottie" cover made of pink organdy fabric and ribbon. Those two things were the hit of the party, the conversation pieces of the evening – HA. My mom just loved the pottie cover.

I still love having parties, especially on lovely summer evenings in Albuquerque. I held parties for many years to celebrate my own birthday. I had them in my backyard, and friends brought potluck dishes and lawn chairs and we had wonderful times. On some occasions I have shown slides of my trips abroad. I did get to see much of the world that I dreamed of as a child. My friend,

Ron, brought his screen and I bought a slide projector. Ron even wrote a poem about me and the lady with the camera.

BEHIND THE LENS

The photos to be within these pages,
Capture a moment along life's stages,
A special landscape, a fiery sky,
A flock of birds, just winging by.
A gurgling brook, a clear blue lake,
A snowy mountain, a birthday cake.
It might be "Big Foot" or a neighbor's cat,
A deer in the forest, an old floppy hat.
There might be some characters you're happy to see,
It might be you or it might be me.
Whatever the subject, whatever the blurbs,
"A picture is worth a thousand words."
So as you peruse from beginning to end,
And ponder these pictures of nature and friends,
Remember the person and camera she tends,
T'was Betty Smith behind the lens.

R. W. Nelson

I bought a good Canon camera in the late 70's and took a couple of photography courses. One was an evening course at the University of New Mexico. My dear husband, Ray, went with me because he did not want me on campus alone at night – even way back then. After he left in '82, I joined the NM Mountain Club and a singles group after that, both of which centered around trips and hikes all around the Southwest.

LIVING LIFE TO THE FULLEST

I have taken many beautiful shots of wildflowers, mountains and rivers on our trips. In the fall of 1998, I took a picture of a brilliant, red Virginia Creeper growing over huge cut on an old Russian Olive tree by my back patio. I never thought of winning a prize at the time, but the next year the New Mexico Museum of Natural History had a photo contest and so, I entered the photo. When I received the letter that I had won First Place, I could not believe it.

There was a reception at the Museum, and I invited several friends. The Photography Show coordinator and host for the reception said that I had more friends there than any of the other participants. I received a crisp one hundred dollar bill for my prize – better than a certificate!!!! HA! The museum enlarged my picture and hung it with previous years' winners. I said that I was a museum piece.

In Albuquerque, one of my favorite memories is attending Trinity United Methodist Church. When I was graduating from college and coming out to Arizona and New Mexico to teach, a friend in college was from Albuquerque. She told me that if I were ever in Albuquerque, I should go to Trinity, since that was the church where she grew up and her parents still attended. So that is why I knew about the church. I went there when I came into town from the Reservation and, then, was married there. Later, when we moved to Albuquerque in 1970, Ray and I started attending.

It was a wonderful place for us, since there were many other couples our age and we had such great times together. We made our first Albuquerque friends there, some of whom I still count as friends. It was a rather large church then, but the people were friendly. Ray was Episcopalian, but everyone there just accepted him as a regular member. He really enjoyed it and sometimes ushered. He always seemed happy and at ease there. We often had spaghetti suppers and he helped out in the kitchen with the other guys. In the fall, we always had a "Roundup" to get people back after vacations. We played games and ate wonderful Bar-B-Que.

In the mid 70's, we had a new church secretary, Cheryl, who married a teacher named Don. Don had led trips in the wilderness of northern New Mexico and knew the outdoors quite well. They began organizing all-church camping trips. Trips were always planned for the week after school was out, since several of us were teachers and ready to get away at the end of school. For many years we went to the Santa Clara Indian Reservation, high up in the mountains northwest of Santa Fe. It was at 9,000 feet altitude with three lakes that stretched out along a twelve-mile dirt road.

We camped beside a little stream under the tall pines in a little emerald green meadow. The first years Ray and I had a little tent. Others had campers or RVs. Later, I had a small Dodge truck with a shell on the back. It was all carpeted with storage boxes along the side – very nice and clean. I loved to come back there after hiking up and down the stream. I opened the little windows along the side and took a nap listening to the rippling stream with the cool breeze floating across my face.

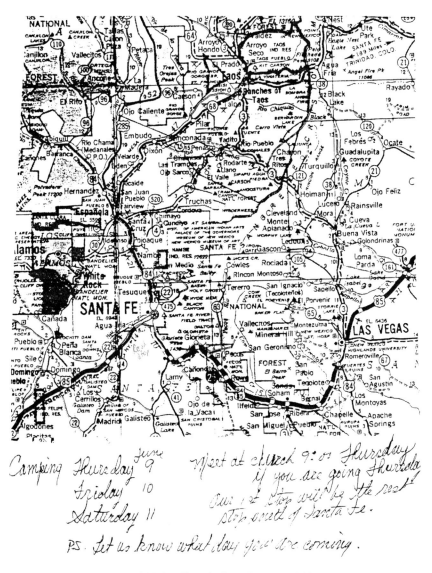

Map Trinity Church Camping, June 1994

ANTELOPE RUNNING

There were wild flowers blooming by June, including fragile, wild, pink roses. We camped between the second and third lake, and sometimes hiked up to the third one. Once we saw beautiful, little, purple shooting stars and a yellow lady's slipper. Someone brought horseshoes and games for the children. At suppertime we spread out delicious potluck dishes on a table. After supper, about sundown, we walked about a quarter of a mile up to the beaver pond. We told the children they must be very quiet, but the beavers would hear us anyway, flap their big, flat tails on the water as signal of danger and dive under. After that we went back to camp, sat around the campfire and sang old songs to the soft strum of Cheryl's guitar. We sang "oldies" like "She'll Be Coming around the Mountain," "On Top of Old Smokey," "Shine on Harvest Moon," and more.

The next morning I got up early and went for a walk about sunrise. Sometimes on the way back I met Susan, a dear friend. When I returned, Tom or another guy had started the campfire and the coffee water boiling. By this time, others were up making breakfast – bacon frying in the crisp mountain air with scrambled eggs and green chili. I can still almost taste those delicious eggs. Sometimes M. or Virginia, both of whom were in campers, invited me in for coffee later. This was pretty close to paradise for me as I had learned to love nature – the woods, flowers and wild animals – I think I modeled my mother as she loved them too.

Susan and I were on the Nurture and Care Committee. We planned activities for the aging congregation. My favorite was down south about eighty five miles to the Bosque del Apache Wildlife Refuge. Watching sunsets behind the distant mountains with V-shaped formations of cranes or Canada geese silhouetted against the glowing clouds are some of my favorite memories. Then we stopped the church van by the Owl Bar in the little town of San Antonio for green chile cheeseburgers. I even had a beer with mine and no one minded.

Ray and I met so many wonderful friends at Trinity, other couples our age. We even took a few trips with some. One unforgettable time, four couples went camping at Chaco Canyon. They were Susan and Cordell, Jean and Ron, Y.C. and Grace and Ray and I. Y.C. and Grace wanted to buy Navajo rugs because they had just bought a home in Sandia Heights. The first night out, which was a Friday, we camped near Crownpoint because there was a Navajo Rug Auction that evening. We camped out near Mariano Lake where I had taken my dog for runs several years earlier when I lived out there. First, we went to the Auction where the Hsus bought rugs.

ANTELOPE RUNNING

CROWNPOINT RUG WEAVERS' ASSOCIATION

RUG AUCTION

AND CHILI SUPPER
FRIDAY
FEBRUARY 17, 1967
CROWNPOINT PUBLIC
SCHOOL

SUPPER 5:00 to 7:00 P. M.

AUCTION 7:30 P. M.

BUYERS: Come early in order to have time to see the rugs before you bid.
SELLERS: Please bring rugs to the Public School the day of the Auction between 2:00 P. M. and 4:00 P. M. Cotton warp rugs will not be accepted.

LIVING LIFE TO THE FULLEST

The next morning we drove on up to Chaco Canyon to explore. I took one of my best photographs of Chaco on that visit. The National Monument had wonderful camp grounds, and we found a perfect one for all of us. There was a rock overhang under which we set up our stove and table. I remember laughing and calling us "cave women" as we prepared our supper "for our men." I was so happy.

Chaco Canyon is a large Anasazi Indian ruin, the largest north of Mexico. The Anasazi were prehistoric Pueblo-type people. The Southwest, including Colorado, is the location of many of these ancient sites. Mesa Verde in the southwest corner of Colorado is another famous large one.

There were hundreds of Indian tribes in the United States. Each had its own language and culture. The Navajo of the Athabascan language group had migrated from southern Canada to the Southwest around the time of Columbus. For many years, they were a nomadic tribe. Later the Spanish brought sheep and silver. The Navajo men became shepherds and silversmiths, while the women were rug weavers. They built hogans for homes and lived in family groups called "camps." Many still live that way, with no electricity or running water.

The Pueblos were agrarian and usually farmed near a water supply for irrigation. The majority are in New Mexico along the Rio Grande River from Taos near the Colorado border to Isleta just south of Albuquerque. Zuni is near a lake south of Gallup, N.M.

Two couples went on another wonderful trip over Labor Day weekend of 1981. Ron and Jean had just bought a new boat. They wanted to go to Lake Powell on the border between northern Arizona and southern Utah. They invited Ray and me to go along.

ANTELOPE RUNNING

We camped on the Utah side at a place called Bull Frog. The next day Ron wanted to take the boat down to Rainbow Bridge, about fifty miles south. Rainbow is a fantastic rock formation where the center has been carved out by erosion. A half-circle of sandstone forms the "rainbow." I am so glad that we did this trip as the Lake is drying up now because of droughts all over the Southwest.

One day we went out so that Ron could water ski. He was so patient and let me try, but I could never get up. I just fell and splashed a lot. Another day, we went up and down the Lake, going in and out of the gorgeous side canyons-red in various shades of sandstone.

One of my favorite stories is about cleaning up after supper one evening. I said that we should save the aluminum foil. Jean said, "Oh, Betty, that's depression syndrome." Now, I think many of us save it because of the environment.—HA!

We took another great trip in the fall of 1983 after my divorce. Cordell, Susan and Paul, their teenage son, and I went to Canyon de Chelley for a weekend. I really appreciated their going as I needed some distraction from my recent problems. They had heard of the Canyon, and they wanted to see it, especially since I talked so much about it.

8

The Later Years

In the mid-1990s, I joined an organization called the American Association of University Women (AAUW). At first I became secretary for the Albuquerque Branch, and later Media Chair at the state level. I write press releases about our upcoming events and work to get the press releases published. I am also Education Chair for the AAUW, Albuquerque Branch. I keep informed through e-mails with the Public Education Department in Santa Fe. My job is to give a written report at branch board meetings and at state-level meetings on media coverage.

In 2003 at a State Leadership Team Meeting in Taos, I proposed that the organization submit a resolution regarding the Patriot Act. The motion was voted on and passed. The Resolution was written and passed again at a State Convention. It was then taken to the National Convention in Providence, Rhode Island in the summer of 2003 where it also passed. The resolution put the AAUW on record opposing imposition on our Civil Rights in the Patriot Act.

In the fall of 2004, I proposed another resolution to be written to the Federal Communications Commission. The resolution covered their duties and responsibilities in overseeing objective coverage in the news media of all important political, social, scientific and environmental issues facing the country. This included full coverage of local, national and world news events. The motion went through the regular channels for approval at State Association meetings of AAUW.

A committee was appointed. The resolution was written and taken to the National Convention in June 2005, where it passed unanimously. It was submitted to the Federal Communications Commission by Lisa Maatz, chair of public relations and government affairs of the national office of AAUW. I was very excited, since the convention was at the Omni Shoreham Hotel where Nancy Pelosi, Democratic Leader in the House of Representatives, was one of our speakers. I was able to shake hands with her and had my picture taken with her.

AAUW NATIONAL CONVENTION
Washington, D.C. – Omni Shoreham Hotel
June 24-27, 2005

Federal Communications Commission Resolution

Resolve that the American Association of University Women request that the Federal Communications Commission (FCC) exercise its powers over all broadcast licensees to assure the fair presentation of objective coverage and discussion of all important political, social, scientific and environmental issues facing the country including full coverage of local, national and world events.

Further resolve that the American Association of University

Women request that the Federal Communications Commission (FCC) cease drafting new rules which would permit greater consolidation of broadcast media which would control the amount of comprehensive news coverage available to the citizens of this country.

I had a knowledgeable committee here in Albuquerque who worked on this including a former executive with CBS; he was the husband of one of our AAUW members.

As media chair at the state level and education chair for the Albuquerque Branch, I attend meetings in Santa Fe of the Legislative Education Study Committee, an interim committee which meets year-round to discuss pertinent issues related to education and prepare proposals for submission to the State Legislature the following January.

I also serve on the AAUW Lobby Corps where we visit our legislators during the session to ask for their votes on issues concerning education, childcare, women and domestic violence and pay equity for women. All of these issues are of great interest to me as I am firmly convinced that education is the answer to so many of our social problems. This is surely related to the fact that education was my way up and out of the poverty in which I was born. I am involved in EE, and that does not mean electrical engineer. It stands for Education and the Environment. I have been active in environmental groups for about the last fifteen years. We started working on global warming/climate change in the mid-90s with the New Mexico Conference of Churches. It has been my pleasure to see the Public Utilities Company of New Mexico go in a forward direction on climate change by installing wind towers on the plains of eastern New Mexico.

1983 was quite an eventful year for me. My divorce was final. I went on a dream-come-true vacation to Spain, Portugal and Morocco. When I returned, I housed a foreign exchange student from Sweden. We had a party in my backyard where guests brought food from all over the world. My former neighbors, Jake and Virginia, who was Philippino, brought the biggest platter of egg rolls that I have ever seen. A friend's husband who was a chef helped me make paella, the Spanish dish with seafood, and he brought apple strudel from Austria, his home. Another friend, formerly from Baghdad, brought tabouleh, made with bulgur wheat, chopped tomatoes and lemon juice.

That fall of 1983, I went to a very helpful Divorce Recovery Seminar where I met so many nice people. About that same time, a friend told me about the New Mexico Mountain Club. This is a fabulous group of about 700 lovers of the outdoors. I have always been one of those people, since I grew up on a black-land farm in North Texas where I walked the stream banks every spring, went fishing and hunting with my older brother. I remember the fragile, little Johnny-Jump-Ups and the purple violets creeping up through the thick layer of dead leaves from the previous fall.

In the Mountain Club, I made wonderful friends, some of whom I still have. I hiked and camped over much of New Mexico, especially the northern part. We also hiked in Colorado and Arizona, including the Grand Canyon. At the Grand Canyon, we went down the six-mile Kaibab Trail, spent the night at Phantom Ranch along the Colorado River, and hiked back up ten miles on Bright Angel Trail the next day. I still recall a small herd of deer we saw down by the river that evening.

I became a leader in the club leading Class I hikes in Albuquerque's Sandia and Manzano Mountains. I also served on the board as conservation chair and librarian. I still remember one particular walk in the Sandia foothills on a bright, sunny Saturday morning. We had a light snow the previous night and it just glistened in the early sunlight. I recall another hike in the Sandias where we had a light shower and there was a rainbow. I had never been so close to a rainbow before and it looked as if we could hike to the end and find the "pot of gold."

I went on many trips and learned much of the 200 miles of trails in the Sandias. One Sunday afternoon we were on the east side, pretty high up. It must have been during our "monsoon season" in the summer. The rain came in a hard downpour, and the thunder and lightening were frightening.

We were not far from the rim, and one minute we could see the lights of Albuquerque below, and the next minute, all the lights were out, jet black. This was the time a VW was washed over a bridge and into an arroyo or ditch. The water rushes down the mountain so fast it catches people off guard. Kids play in the concrete ditches and are sometimes swept away. Some drown if they're not rescued by the Fire Department.

We also hiked many times in the Pecos Wilderness northeast of Santa Fe. Windsor Trail from the Santa Fe Ski Basin was one of my favorites where we went four miles up to a plateau-like area called Puerto Nambe. We could look across and see Santa Fe Baldy Mountain. We did that in early October, and I took one of my best pictures of Baldy with an early snow framed by golden aspen. It hangs in my den now.

One of my last hikes before serious back surgery was in that area up to Hamilton Mesa leaving from Iron Gate Campground. That area is known for terrific summer storms and it came in a downpour. The trails were like rivers and another gal and I could not keep up as other hikers were running. We missed a turnoff and became lost. It was very scary as that is also black bear country, and I was thinking we might have to spend the night in the mountains. I told the other lady if we keep going south, we will be parallel with the road.

After about a mile or so, we could see shiny metal on parked cars to our right. So, we just started bushwhacking down the mountain (no trail) and arrived at the forest road. We walked a short distance and met our people leaving from the hike. They told us that Search and Rescue were out looking for us. In a few minutes here they came up the road with horses to go out and look for us. Of course, I was pretty happy to be down with no night in the wilderness. The Stamms, Bill and Ruth, were leading that hike and had sent for Search and Rescue. I remember sitting up on the Mesa during lunch, and we could see the storm clouds gathering. Quite dramatic, but of course we had no idea what was to come later that afternoon.

Another unforgettable trip was with the Masons down to the Organ Mountains east of Las Cruces, New Mexico. The sunset was gorgeous from our campsite. One more similar one was with my friend, Fran Koski, down to Three Rivers State Park near the lava beds southeast of Albuquerque. We went to an old ghost town called Live Oak where we were able to tour an old-fashioned school house. It reminded me of the one where I went to elementary school in North Texas. The desks were the same, with the inkwell hole on the right side. Older people talked about how boys who sat behind girls dipped their pigtails in the inkwells. This never happened to me, since we did not use the inkwells. We wrote with pencils.

The Masons lead a great trip to La Plata Canyon in Colorado, west of Durango. We stayed at a campsite there. The next morning we piled into four-wheel drive vehicles and drove on up to a trail head. It was very high, so we could look northwest and see much higher peaks such as Mt. Wilson. We hiked west from there through trails that were too rough for me to keep up. It was alright though as I saw cute little marmots and pikas. Sunday morning was quite exciting as a bear was rummaging through the garbage cans in the campground. I was very glad a friend had invited me to share her camper truck the night before, since my tent leaked.

Another friend I met in the Club, Mary Jane, and I went on many sunset picnics in Elena Gallegos Open Space area in the Sandia foothills on the west side, a few miles from my house. Sometimes after a hike, we wanted a steak, so we just went up to the County Line Restaurant, nearby. We did not even mind waiting for a table as we could go in the bar and have a margarita.

I went on the longest hike that I ever did with this group. We were in the San Pedro Parks Wilderness Area in northwestern New Mexico, north of the small town of Cuba. Bill and Ruth Stamm were leading this one, too. We started at the San Gregorio Lake Trailhead. It was only a mile up to the Lake which was a beautiful, high-mountain lake with purple iris growing over in the northwest corner. We hiked way past that, about five miles, up to a high plateau with grassy meadows. I remember hiking along a quiet, little stream on the way back. It was eleven miles round trip. I lost a sweater, but some friends behind me found it. This was the first time that anyone mentioned to me that I should write my story. I was telling Carolyn about teaching on the Navajo Indian Reservation. She suggested that I write about it, and now I am doing just that. Carolyn was a librarian at the Zinn Library at the University of New Mexico. Thank you, Carolyn.

ANTELOPE RUNNING

I belonged to another outdoor hiking group, Outdoor Adventures for Singles. I had wonderful trips with them, too. One of my favorites was to the Grand Canyon again. We went to the west end, to the Havasupai Trail down to the Supai Indian Reservation. I had heard of this trail many years before. It is famous for its gorgeous turquoise pools near the Reservation. The beautiful travertine rock drapes the sides. I drove my "new" little Dodge Ram camper truck, and a new friend went with me. She had recorded two tapes of Carlos Nakai, the Navajo flute player, for us to play on the long drive. After we turned off the highway on the road leading to the trailhead, I played one of those tapes, "Canyon Trilogy." It was very mystic as I could just imagine an Indian up on one of those mountains playing that flute.

I took another trip with this group to the Churicaca National Forest in southeastern Arizona. I drove my Pontiac Phoenix with a friend named H.P. We went south on I-25 and then west on I-10 through Lordsburg, New Mexico and into Arizona. It was beautiful rugged mountain terrain, only about fifty miles from the Mexican border. There were tropical birds there, although I did not see any. We visited an old rancher's home that was quite interesting.

One of my most enjoyable trips with this group was river rafting on the Green River in northern Utah. I rode up with C. and two other friends. We left on my birthday, June 1st. I told them after they picked me up that it was "my day." We then turned around and went back to one of the homes to get birthday candles. We stopped for lunch in Mesa Verde National Park, west of Durango, Colorado. Someone had made chocolate brownies, and so I had a blue birthday candle on a brownie. I thought it doesn't get any better than this. I was so happy that day. I had always wanted to dance on a table, and that day I did; someone took my picture on the picnic table. These outdoor groups were "laid back," so I had fabulous times with them.

We drove on to Telluride, Colorado, where we pitched our tents out west of town. That evening for dinner, we went into town to a steak place where I had been previously. After a wonderful dinner, I ordered the biggest chocolate sundae I have ever seen. I also, asked for eleven spoons, and we all shared it. I was very happy then, too.

The next day we drove on to Price, Utah where we met professors and staff from the College of Eastern Utah. They were our guides on the rafting trip. We piled into vans and drove further north to get to the river. We launched the rafts at a small place called Sand Wash, a few miles south of the Wyoming border. It was a bright, sunny day – just perfect for a day on the river. The water became rough though, and I fell overboard. I crawled back in the boat with some help. They just pulled me in like a big sack of potatoes. Other younger rafters than I fell overboard, too, so I did not feel so bad. One does not concern oneself with being graceful at a time like that.

We camped under the cottonwoods. The crew grilled steaks to order that first evening for dinner. This was a four-day trip with only thirty one people, many of whom were college students who got credit on their environmental degree for the trip. The kids helped me load my big sea bag on the oar boat every morning after I had stuffed all my gear into it.

The fourth day was on Class-IV rapids. I rode in the oar boat with all the equipment, and did not need to worry about falling overboard. A group of Boy Scouts had drowned there a few years before. We disembarked at the town of Green River, went back to Price to get our own car. Then we headed south and passed by where the Green River runs into the Colorado River. From there we continued on to Arches National Monument in southern Utah where we hiked around and took pictures. Then we drove on into Arizona, past Mexican Hat and on to Canyon de Chelley. I have traveled quite a few foreign countries on fabulous trips, but this was one of my favorites.

One reason I had a great time on the Green River Trip was because a certain guy, who will remain anonymous, was on the trip. We were not dating at that time, but we rode up with another guy and gal. One evening some of the group was playing horseshoes on the sandy river beach. I passed, since I've never been very good at horseshoes, and maybe "the tall one" was not either. It worked out just as I had hoped. We went for a nice walk in the evening sunset.

Later we began to date. One of our traditions was to take each other out to dinner for our birthdays. We went hiking and camping after that as we both loved the outdoors. We never went to a movie. One beautiful spring morning we both took our cameras and went to the east side of the Sandia Mountains and took pictures of wildflowers. We then went by and picked up barbecue ribs, and went to his house and looked at the pictures on his computer. Sometimes when I visited him, I came home with fresh corn-on-the-cob, since he always had a garden.

Since 1983 when I was still teaching full time, I've had the habit of exercise. During the fall of '83, I began walking twelve blocks before I went to school. After school I went to water aerobics three times a week at 6:00 p.m. I still walk my dog almost every day and do water aerobics three times a week at 8:00 a.m.

THE LATER YEARS

I have gone to a lovely retreat center on the west side of Albuquerque near the Rio Grande River. I have done Yoga and Tai Chi classes over there. One lovely, moonlit, late, summer evening, we had a yoga class in the foothills of the Sandia Mountains. By this time I was not hiking up that mountain the way I had done years earlier. I was trudging up with my yoga mat and other gear, when a young woman came up behind me in a hurry. She asked if she could help carry something. She said she was running late, since she had just had a baby who was back at the trailhead with his dad. I finally made it up to the group site and completed the rest of the class.

We gathered up everything and started walking back. I walked beside the woman who had helped me carry things. I asked, "What is the baby's name?" She replied, "Joaquin." I said, "Oh, I used to know a funny guy whose name was Joaquin where I worked in Dallas." Not thinking it was relevant, I mumbled "At the Cotton Exchange." She asked, "Esteve Brothers?" I was so surprised. I told her that was right. Turns out her husband, Joe, is related to the Esteve Family on his mother's side. We had a big hug and Katy and Joe have since become some of my best friends. They are so kind and good to me. We go out to eat and rotate who picks up the check. They are now on my emergency call list.

I volunteer with two great outdoor conservation groups. One is the United States Forest Service. I have had hours of training as an Interpreter, and during the summer, I work up at the top of the Tram at the Forest Service Visitor Center desk in the Sandia Mountains. We greet people, help to answer their questions about the Mountain, and give out trail maps if they wish to hike. I have hiked most of the trails and have done nature walks up there. We have a Junior Ranger Program, and I help parents and children with the program. The parents take the children on the quarter-mile nature walk, read the signs describing that location; each child does a worksheet, brings it back and we give them a "Junior Ranger" badge or patch for their pack or jacket.

In addition I do "deck talks" outside where I talk about basic geology of the Mountain along with describing the plant and animal life. I started this in the early 90's and look forward to it every summer when I go up once a week. The Visitor Center is closed in the winter. I have met so many interesting people from all over the world. Some ask to take my picture, since I wear a U.S. Forest Service uniform and a cowboy hat. One day when I was still leading nature walks, I had four young men from Germany. Only one of them spoke English, so he interpreted for me.

When we have plenty of rain, the wild flowers are so gorgeous. At 10,000 feet + altitude, the vegetation is plentiful. Some of my favorite flowers are purple Penstemon and red/orange columbine, a fragile little flower. Another one is the Calypso Orchid or Ladies Slipper. It is a delicate little pink flower that does not grow very tall, maybe eight or 10 inches at the most. It likes the damp soil near a stream or in the shade of a big conifer tree (fir or spruce).

I also volunteer with the Rio Grande Nature Center which is in the center of Albuquerque along the River. I have been there since the spring of 1990 when a friend and I went there for training. At the end of the training, I received a beautiful photograph of the Chama River in northwestern New Mexico. This has been another exciting experience. It is located in what is called "the Bosque" which, in Spanish, means woods along the river. The area is covered with huge old Rio Grande cottonwood trees which are another species different from the Prairie cottonwood. The place is like a golden cathedral in October when the cottonwoods turn yellow. There are nature trails where I led walks over to the river several years ago. A well-designed visitor center with an observation pond is part of the Center. People can sit and watch various species of ducks and other wildfowl glide over the pond and land to have breakfast. There is a small island where one morning I spotted a Canada goose with five furry little yellow babies.

Another fun event I work at the Nature Center is the Festivals. We have the "Wings Festival" where hummingbirds, butterflies and dragonflies are celebrated. I preside over a table called the "Bosque Bits" that has bird wings, hummingbird bills, nests and other specialties for visitors – especially children – to look at and learn to appreciate nature. Arts and crafts are for sale in one section, plants for sale in another place, and a children's activities table. Sometimes my table is located right beside the cookies and lemonade stand. Families come with children of all ages, sometimes people in wheel chairs venture out with family. One perfectly lovely Saturday morning as I walked in, someone was playing a CD, a beautiful song by Andrea Bocelli, one of my favorite artists.

In the late 1990's I belonged to an organization, New Mexico Friends of the Forest, now called Friends of the Sandia Mountains. I wrote a column for our monthly newsletter, and here is a poem that I wrote for the October 1999 publication.

T'was the summer of 99

Walks by the lake as
smooth as glass,

Bordered by snow-covered
14,000 foot peaks,

A straight aspen walking
stick which I kept

The long road north through
the San Luis Valley,

THE LATER YEARS

With the Crestone Mountains
in the East and the San
Juans to the West

Fields of wild iris along
the roadside,

A rippling stream running
parallel with
the winding road,

Peaceful green pastures
With cattle and horses grazing,

Then there's the Santa Fe
Ski Basin on a misty day,

Counting purple shooting stars,
elephant heads and fireweed.

The enduring enchantment of the
Sandias—Tecolote (owl)
Trail by moonlight,

The moon on the horizon like
a big orange beach ball,

Reading Navajo and Pueblo poetry
by moonlight,

ANTELOPE RUNNING

Composing an imaginary salad
with mountain parsley and
wild mushrooms found along the trail.
It was the year of the purple
penstemon

in the Sandias—meadows of
them—and purple asters and
harebells.

A late afternoon wedding in a
field of sunflowers beside
a small pond,

The spectacular cloud formations
against the azure sky.

I must record it—etch it in my mind.

An example of the kindness of the Indian people, about five years ago I came around a corner of an aisle in Home Depot, and this big guy said, "Hello, Mrs. Smith." I said, "I am sorry, but I don't know your name." He said, "I'm Edwin L. I was in your fourth grade class at Isleta Pueblo." We hugged and talked for a few minutes. He gave me his card, and I gave him mine. He said he was the manager of the Isleta Casino.

A few months later during the Christmas holidays, I received a Christmas card from him at the Casino. He invited me to come out there for dinner some evening after Christmas. He said he wanted to take his fourth grade teacher to dinner. Of course I was delighted. He asked me to meet him upstairs in the fine dining room. When I told the head waiter who I was, he ushered me over to a reserved table. Then Edwin came in. The waiter brought over a beautiful yellow rose, and we had a delicious dinner. What a delightful surprise!

I believe that I was a good teacher, but do not consider myself an expert at much else. I do like this Nigerian Proverb that I ran across, recently:

If you can walk, you can dance

If you can talk, you can sing!

I could never win any dance contests, but I did love to dance when I was young. I cannot sing very well unless I am sitting by someone who can so that I can follow.

My thanks to my family and good friends who believed in me; and, so, I have been able to "dance and sing" much of my life. As the author, William James, said:

"Wherever you are, it is your friends who make your world."

My friends in my neighborhood on my same block have been so incredible to me, truly more than just good neighbors. Jerry and Valerie — Valerie is a nurse and was my nurse during back surgery several years ago. Jerry, her husband, is my "Computer Tech." When I have a problem, he has saved me hundreds of dollars.

Chris and Lois and children- Chris is a landscape artist and has done my yard in xeriscape, and takes care of it on a regular basis. He does not charge me regular price and, when, I mention this, he just says, "That's a neighbor discount." The children take my dog for a walk when I don't have time or feel like it.

Stewart and Camille - I have known them for more than thirty-five years. They keep my dog and watch my house when I am out of town. They are on my emergency call list, and have said that I may call in the middle of the night if necessary.

Big thanks to my friend, Audrey, who first told me about the Rio Grande Nature Center. We went there as volunteers and did the interpreters' six weeks of training in the spring of 1990; I have been a volunteer there ever since. She also introduced me to SouthWest Writers, a writing group that has been invaluable to me.

⚛

It is Thanksgiving weekend, 2009, and I am looking forward to boarding the big jet plane for Dallas and Christmas with the family. I always stay with Jo, my youngest sister. She meets me at the airport, either with Mary, our other sister, or we go pick her up at her home. Then we all go to Jo's lovely home, and the three sisters are together for a few days. We go shopping for some of the food, but the ham and turkey have already been ordered. It is such a wonderful time for us to be together and reminisce about long ago.

Jo has a tree up, and her home is decorated beautifully. She may have friends over for dinner or drinks before Christmas.

On Christmas Eve, we dress up and go over to one of my nephew's home for an all family get-together. All the nieces and nephews are there with their children. My brother, Jack, has six great grand-children. Presents are exchanged with the children, and toys and wrapping paper have to be carefully stepped around. There is plenty of food and drink and wonderful "catching up" to do.

The next day, Christmas, Mary, Jo and I exchange gifts first thing in the morning. Then Jo fixes a delicious breakfast of scrambled eggs, bacon or sausage, and hot biscuits. After that, we get dressed and start cooking. Jo has put the turkey on early, probably 6:00 a.m. Mary always makes the dressing, and has brought a great, green chile, corn casserole. My part is to fix the fresh cranberries and fruit salad.

Liesel, Jo's daughter, Tracie, Mary's daughter and Chris, another niece and other members of the family come in, and we have a feast. Later, Jack and his sons come by in the afternoon. It is a great family time.

I feel extremely blessed that I "chose" to be a part of this fabulous family, and will always treasure it. No matter where I travel or what experiences I have.

My Family, c. 1975 (Dad had previously passed away)
Back Row, L. to R. Betty, Dick, Bob, Jack, Hazel
Front Row: Mary, our Mom, Jo

Acknowledgements

Rob Spiegel - My Patient Editor, Southwest Writers Workshop (SWW)

Larry Greenly - My Technical Advisor, Southwest Writers Workshop (SWW)

Jerry Boatwright - My Computer Tech and Neighbor

Carolyn Dodson - Friend who first suggested that I should write about teaching on the Indian Reservations now many years ago

Joan Rogers, Author Representative, Outskirts Press, Denver, Colorado

LaVergne, TN USA
05 September 2010
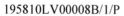
195810LV00008B/1/P